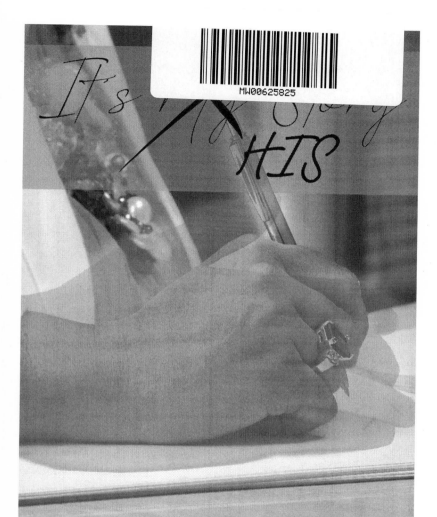

*It's My Story/HIS*

*HIS*

*"Encouragement to Worship While Wounded"*

# Dr. LaSonja Flowers-Ivory

*Foreword by Wanda Bolton-Davis*

## It's My Story; It's His Story

© Copyright 2019 by LaSonja Flowers-Ivory
Ivory Educational Publishing

ISBN: 978-1-7335796-0-5
Library of Congress Control Number: 2019900208

Cover Design, Logo, and Photography
CIR Design • www.cir-design.com

Editing and Formatting
www.affordablechristianediting.com

Printed in the United States of America

# Dedication

To SHAWNA OLIVER, the daughter God sent to me. While I did not have the honor of giving birth to you, God gives me the privilege of hearing you call me "Mom."

# Acknowledgments

To my husband and primary earthly focus, Eric. Thank you for allowing me to be me. While much of your support is silent, it is very active. Being married to you gave me the additional courage, confidence and time to devote myself to writing this book and starting our business. Your love stabilizes me and makes me want to be a better person.

# Special Thanks

I MUST EXTEND both my love and gratitude to all who have allowed me to serve as their Bible teacher, particularly Ruth Ayala Ramirez, Veronica Davis, and Tracy Howard. Many of you took the time to consistently encourage me by sharing the impact of the Word of God in your personal lives. This section would be pages long if I listed all of your names, but I see your faces as I type this acknowledgment. And you know who you are. Your attendance, questions, challenges, testimonies, and growth contributed to this book.

Thank you...

To my children, for periodically reminding me of the positive impact I have made to your lives. You were the first students God entrusted me to teach, and I learned a lot from you. Since I can't go back and fix the mistakes I made with you, I will make sure your children reap the benefits of my learning.

To my mother, Marie Flowers, for giving me your best.

To my new parents, Willie and Lafray Ivory, for your love and acceptance.

To my siblings, Trecia, Bivin, and Janda, for supporting in your own way.

To Wanda Bolton Davis, for more than twenty years

of friendship and opportunities to share my gift and purpose.

To Linda Stubblefield for providing excellent editorial services. You were more than an editor.

To Miles Robinson for the cover design and business logo.

To Carla Freeman for makeup on the cover design.

To Takai by Angela for the jewelry on the cover design.

To Fred Hammond, my favorite Gospel artist. We have never met, but God used your music as part of my healing and encouragement to continue to trust, fight, and pray.

A separate book would be required to detail how each of you have impacted my life, so for now...special thanks because your lives have enriched mine:

Shelly Brody

Paula Brown

Adrienne Cooper

Frances Donison

Nakia Flowers Hall

Melanie Infante

Cynthia Kimble

Kimberly McGary

Katie McKarrel

Dr. Irene Pinkard

Bobbie Richards

Patrice Robinson

Shena Sanchez

# Table of Contents

# Foreword

Too often those who proclaim the Gospel, teach a distorted message that once an individual makes the choice to live for Jesus Christ, his or her life will become easier. It would be wonderful if that were true. However, in reality, it is the opposite. Christianity does not exempt us from the painful places in life; in fact, Christianity can be viewed as a purposeful invitation to embark upon a journey that may sometimes open the door for painful places. There is no way around it. Life is hard, life hurts, and life is full of pain. As a result, all of us have a story to tell.

As I read this inspiring book, the famous African American hymn written by Jennie Wilson came to mind, "Hold to God's Unchanging Hand." Wilson writes, "Time is filled with swift transitions, naught of earth unmoved can stand, build your hopes on things eternal, hold to God's unchanging hand." As a young girl, I did not understand what "swift transitions" meant. However, as an adult, I have lived swift transitions. Our life stories are interwoven through a series of changes—ups and downs, good and bad, joy and sorrow, laughter and tears, rejoicing and grieving. We never know what the next day will bring. However, what we do know is that living for Christ ensures every believer that we do not face the journey of life alone, and that we have a companion that has guaranteed that victory awaits us on the other side.

As you read the following pages, you will laugh, you will cry, and above all, you will experience the presence of God. As Dr. LaSonja shares her story, she is real, transparent and engaging. She integrates her life experiences with biblical foundations and practical application, thus permitting every reader to relate and reflect, while being renewed and restored. She uniquely shares and connects glimpses of her life story to the amazing power of the Word and work of God. As Sonja labored over this book, she realized that her story really isn't her story at all; it is His (God's) story. My prayer for every person who reads this book is that each chapter will cause you to see the hand of God upon your swift transitions and know that God is behind the scenes, penning His story through your life. Happy reading!

– Rev. Dr. Wanda Bolton-Davis
Author: *Victorious Disciples: A Practical Guide for
Christian Discipleship and Mentoring*
Executive Director, Victorious Disciples Ministries, Inc.
Cedar Hill, Texas

# To the Reader

I HAVE PRAYED for you since I began the writing aspect of this book. You—yes, you—were the motivation to begin and complete this project. My prayer is that this book will serve as a reminder of the greatness of God. I asked God to use His Word, coupled with sharing His hand in my life to inform or remind you that you are NEVER alone. God has an amazing, unconditional love for you and can enable you not only to survive but also, to thrive in any circumstance.

I know that you are bombarded with a plethora of information and very little time to process it. I encourage you to find time to reflect on the questions I have included in "Operation Meditation" and answer them; doing so will definitely enrich your experience.

I will continue to pray for you. Remember, even in your life…*It's His Story.*

*A testimony is a terrible thing to waste.*

# CHAPTER ONE

# Love Your Neighbor

**M**ARK 12:31, *"The second is this: Love your neighbor as yourself. There is no commandment greater than these."*

*Love*—a word that is often used and sometimes even lightly. Depending on our experiences, love can leave a bad taste in our mouth or a flood of positive memories and feelings. The very word *love* can evoke a myriad of emotions in people. For some, the word puts a smile on their faces; for others, the word creates pain and provoke tears. A plethora of songwriters and singers have given us heartfelt words of love that link us to the travail of their own hearts and touch the souls of listeners. The themes range from adapting the words of great poets like Elizabeth Barrett Browning, who exquisitely penned, "How do I love thee? Let me count the ways" to Tina Turner's question, "What's love got to do with it?"

I truly believe you could add to the two I have listed and help me write this chapter. Depending on the translation of the Bible consulted, the word love is a topic addressed anywhere from 131 to 319 times. John 3:16 (KJV) states, *"For God so loved the world, that he gave his only begotten Son, that whosoever believeth on him should not perish, but have everlasting life."* Something about this word *love* is indescribable.

John 15:13, *"Greater love has no one than this: to lay down one's life for one's friends."* In addition to God's lovingly demonstrating His love for you, He explicitedly commands us to love Him.

*"And thou shalt love the Lord thy God with all thy heart, and with all thy soul, and with all thy mind, and with all thy strength: this is the first commandment. [31] And the second is like, namely this, Thou shalt love thy neighbour as thyself"* (Mark 12:30, 31 KJV).

*In addition to God's lovingly demonstrating His love for you, He explicitedly commands us to love Him.*

According to the Word of God, we are to love our neighbor, respect others, and regard their needs and desires as highly as we regard our own. On the surface, this command to love our neighbor, which is repeated in Matthew 22:36-40, sounds easier than loving our enemy, right? Well, that judgment would depend on our personal definitions of the word neighbor. If you are anything like me, you may think *friend* when you read the word *neighbor* but stay tuned…that's definitely not God's definition! Loving your neighbor is a command; it is not an option.

I have read and heard this Scripture a hundred times and have even recited it, but I did not pay close attention to the last part of the verse. In this passage, Jesus is neither recommending nor suggesting that we love our neighbor; rather, He is *commanding* us to love our neighbor. Because God has given us the gift of free will, we have the option of not loving, which is disobedience and is also known as sin. Contrary to popular opinion, the word *love* is still very powerful and important because God says so.

When my sons were toddlers, they enjoyed reading several books. One of their favorites was a children's book by P. D. Eastman published by Random House Books. In this book, a chick hatches and walks around looking for its mother. The chick encountered several animals and asked all of them, "Are you my mother?" Of course, all the animals replied no and kindly informed the chick of their identity. The story is very cute and educational.

I feel relatively sure you are probably thinking, *What does this children's book have to do with anything?*

Well, the book reminded me of my thought process as I studied Mark 12:30 and 31. Once I understood what God was commanding—not asking me—my memory replayed a video library of faces one at a time, and I, unlike the chick's asking, "Are you my mother?" began asking "Are you my neighbor?"

Then I re-read Luke 10:25-37.

*On one occasion an expert in the law stood up to test Jesus. "Teacher," he asked, "what must I do to inherit eternal life?"*

*[26]"What is written in the Law?" He [Jesus] replied. "How do you read it?"*

*[27]He answered, "Love the Lord your God with all your heart and with all your soul and with all your strength and with all your mind; and, 'Love your neighbor as yourself.'"*

<sup>28</sup>*"You have answered correctly," Jesus replied. "Do this and you will live."*

<sup>29</sup>*But he wanted to justify himself, so he asked Jesus, "And who is my neighbor?"*

<sup>30</sup>*In reply Jesus said: "A man was going down from Jerusalem to Jericho, when he was attacked by robbers. They stripped him of his clothes, beat him and went away, leaving him half dead. <sup>31</sup>A priest happened to be going down the same road, and when he saw the man, he passed by on the other side. <sup>32</sup>So too, a Levite, when he came to the place and saw him, passed by on the other side. <sup>33</sup>But a Samaritan, as he traveled, came where the man was; and when he saw him, he took pity on him. <sup>34</sup>He went to him and bandaged his wounds, pouring on oil and wine. Then he put the man on his own donkey, brought him to an inn and took care of him. <sup>35</sup>The next day he took out two denari and gave them to an inn and took care of him. The next day he took out two denarii and gave them to the innkeeper. 'Look after him,' he said, 'and when I return, I will reimburse you for any extra expense you may have.'*

<sup>36</sup>*"Which of these three do you think was a neighbor to the man who fell into the hands of robbers?"*

<sup>37</sup>*The expert in the law replied, "The one who had mercy on him." Jesus told him, "Go and do likewise."*

I can relate to the expert in the law. When I read the Scripture commanding me to love my neighbor as myself, I too looked for a loophole. I remember thinking as if I were in a spelling bee, *May I have the definition of "neighbor," please?* I confess; following God's command was a real struggle for me. I was trying to find a way to select my "neighbors." I began to categorize the faces that flashed before me and even created two categories: "Neighbor" and "Never." I reluctantly moved some people to the "neighbor" category, thinking, *Okay, I guess I can love them.* The other category, I (without any biblical grounds) told myself, "God would never expect me to love them."

This temporary, self-hypnosis worked for only a minute because I was reminded of James 1:23-25, which says the following:

> *"Anyone who listens to the word but does not do what it says is like someone who looks at his face in a mirror* <sup>24</sup>*and, after looking at himself, goes away and immediately forgets what he looks like.* <sup>25</sup>*But whosoever looks intently into the perfect law that gives freedom, and continues in it—not forgetting what they have heard, but doing it—they will be blessed in what they do."*

Sometime later, I was teaching a Bible lesson on this Scripture to my women's Sunday school class, and one of my students asked a question much like the expert in the law. "What if you don't know their names, and you only remember their faces—like the person who cut me off on the freeway last week and looked at me without apologizing. He's not my neighbor—right?"

She continued, "My kids were in the car, and he could have

killed us! He was driving really fast, and God knows I don't play when it comes to my kids."

Although the class erupted with laughter at the animation of our dear sister, I could see the mental wheels of others turning. She was not the only one asking for the exception clause. The questions then began like fireworks exploding:

- "What about my mom who has been on drugs all of my life? I watched her take food out of our house, leaving us hungry. She left us home alone for days at a time, and I had to take care of my siblings. I was only eight years old. I saw her come home bruised and beaten and act like everything was normal. Is she my neighbor?"

- "What about my dad who left us, moved in with another woman, and took care of her kids? Is he my neighbor?"

- "What about the family member who molested me? Surely, he is not my neighbor, right?"

- "What about my boss who purposely harasses me? Is she my neighbor?"

- "The husband who has abused me…"

- "The husband who has repeatedly cheated on me…"

- "The person who murdered my sibling…"

- "The children for whom I sacrificed and have now caused me so much pain?"

My students were all staring at me. Finally, Ruth, who had not asked a question, inquired, "Well? Are they all our neighbors?"

I knew the question was rhetorical; that each question was

really a statement was obvious to me. That statement was: *they absolutely cannot be our neighbors.* Jesus could not have been talking about these people; they didn't deserve to be our neighbors. I understood.

The feeling behind each question was fueled by pain; these were genuine people who volunteered to attend this Bible study, and most of them attended consistently. They were struggling with the idea of having to love someone who had desperately hurt them and had caused deep wounds. However, ours was only a 45-minute class, and we needed more time. I invited all who were able to commit to a two-hour session to meet me for an extended study of God's Word and a snapshot of my personal journey on the topic. All of them returned.

If we are not careful, we will believe that what Jesus is asking of us is unfair, unrealistic, and just downright insensitive. I opened the lesson by telling them that I had accepted Christ in June of 1986. Shortly thereafter, I wrote my estranged dad a letter describing the process to him and writing Scriptures for him to read in order to duplicate the process.

I then explained to my students that approximately seven years prior to this day, I had an encounter with God based on this very Scripture. I proceeded to walk them through my journey. I remember asking God, "So let me get this straight, God… You want me to love my biological dad, who I only saw about ten times my whole life, and we lived in the same city? You want me to forgive the man who made promises and never kept them, whose absence created a pain so deep that I developed an unhealthy desire to be loved and accepted?

What about all the birthdays he missed? I made good grades in school—just in case he came around to see my report cards. I even had a special shoebox where I saved them, so I could update him through each year; he never saw them. I hoped for him to visit every holiday—only to be disappointed. My mom was a single mom of four, who did the best she could to provide for us. However, I remember being upset with her when we would move to a different set of apartments. I remember blaming her for James' not being able to find me. The truth is that even when we lived in the same apartments for years, he never visited.

"Lord," I asked, "are You *telling* me to love him—the man who caused me to doubt my self-worth? What about all the years I spent trying to figure out what was wrong with me and what I could do to get him to love me? He's my neighbor? The man I never had a phone number to call? The man whose absence created a yearning for a father that was so deep that I wanted to be the daughter of every "nice" older man I met? God, You saw the tears I shed; this was painful. Lord, You want me to love this man? The unfulfilled gap that resulted from his absence placed me in a dangerous place. Lord, You know all the snares You caused me to avoid. While I was looking for a father-figure, the men to whom I was drawn were not always looking for a daughter. I was not the victim that I could have become, and You are the only reason this story doesn't have a tragic ending. You want me to love this man?

"Oh, and God, let's not forget high school. I was a cheerleader, voted Most Beautiful, first runner-up for Homecoming Queen, and English student of the year. He missed those distinctions. My heart missed him on all those occasions. Is he *really* in the neighbor category?"

I learned in college the psychological effects of an absent father on a daughter. I knew his absenteeism was the root cause of some of my insecurities. "God, what about the pains I felt on each Father's Day, wondering why he didn't want to be with me? I spent years trying to figure out what was wrong with me, remember? I studied several of the girls I knew who had dads in their lives and even tried to imitate them in several ways, hoping I could learn how to gain my dad's attention. These insecurities created a deep fear of rejection; therefore, I made choices to remain in a very unhealthy relationship at a young age.

"So, God, You want me to love the man who created these issues for me? I struggled with being loved unconditionally because of him! Lord, You know better than I do how many barriers this created for YOU and me. Lord, think about all of the work You have had to put in for me to believe that You will never leave me nor forsake me. Is he really my neighbor?"

And God answered, "Yes, he is your neighbor, and yes, I command you to love him."

God's reply was a hard pill for me to swallow, but when is obedience ever easy? God's Word is clear, and when I read John 14:15 (KJV) where Jesus states, *"If ye love me, keep my commandments,"* I knew I had to make a choice. The choice was to obey or disobey, period.

*"If someone says, 'I love God' and hates* [works against] *his brother, he is a liar; for the one who does not love his broth-*

er whom he has seen, cannot love God whom he has not seen (1 John 4:20 NASB). God said that he cannot love a person he has never seen and hate his brother whom he sees every day. If you are anything like me, you are probably thinking, *Well, I don't hate him or her or them.* The point is we must forgive, love, and not look for loopholes when commanded of the Lord.

God is not offended by our questions, especially when we remain in His presence long enough to receive the answers. He has given us His Word to overrule our thoughts and feelings. Psalm 103:14 says, *"for he knows how we are formed, he remembers that we are dust."* God knows our natural tendencies, which is why He tells us to read, study, and hide His Word in our heart. He understands that unless we know what His Word says, we will be governed by our feelings or the words of others.

I cannot emphasize enough the power and strength that comes from knowing and guiding our lives on the principles of God's Word. Paul acknowledges that potential in this way: Romans 7:18 (AMP), *"For I know that nothing good lives in me, that is, in my flesh [my human nature, my worldliness—my sinful capacity]. For the willingness [to do good] is present in me, but the doing of good is not."* I struggled with letting go of this hurt and accepting the reality that God commanded me to love the man who had caused me so much pain. This process was complicated for me for several reasons.

Here's another confession. The word *"commanded"* rubbed me the wrong way. I had not grown up with any structure; therefore, I rarely had to do what anybody told me to do. Believe it or not, I did whatever I wanted to do for the most part in my life. I never had a curfew and frankly, authority figures irritated me. The type of person my dad was created yet another complication.

Let me now introduce you to what I knew of my dad. His name was James, but everyone called him by his nickname— even me. He was tall and handsome with a magnetic personality and a refreshing sense of humor. He had many friends, and people were happy to see him walk into a room. My opinion of James wasn't that he was bad person at all. I had never seen him angry nor did I ever hear him say a negative word about anyone. Whenever he did come around, I loved being in his presence, and I was also very sad when he would leave. I did love him, but I also had some strong, negative feelings for him. For years I did not know how to balance these emotions. After many prayers, sermons, music therapy (nothing formal, just listening to cassettes and CDs) and reading God's Word, I eventually decided to obey what God had been telling me to do. My heart felt so much lighter and doing something simply because God said to felt good. I was happy that I knew how to do something that pleased God. This experience taught me much about myself and God; it was also preparation for the life ahead of me.

However, many events transpired before I reached that point. When I turned 21, I began in earnest to search for my dad. I drove to the address to where I had sent the letter five years earlier, but I found he no longer lived there. I left my phone number with someone who saw him occasionally. When he eventually called, I shared with him that I was getting married in a few months and desired for him to attend and give me away. He accepted and agreed to send his measurements to me (before the days of everything being done online).

I was excited because my wedding would be the first special occasion we would spend together. *Finally, after all the imagined events, I would have a real father-daughter experience.* I felt like I was eight years old. I went to visit my mom and two of my siblings were there. When I excitedly shared the news, I could not believe that I was the only one who was happy. My mom felt betrayed; in her opinion, he had not earned the privilege of escorting me down the aisle, and she was upset with me for making the offer.

My brother was upset as well; he too believed that my dad did not deserve this honor. "Sonja, how could you ask him to give you away? He has never been here for you. I have been here for you more than he has. If anyone is going to give you away, it should be me! If you let him give you away, I will not be there," my brother exclaimed.

I was confused; my emotions went from ecstatic to angry within seconds. Questions shot through my mind. *How can they be upset with me? How can they not want me to experience this once-in-a-lifetime bliss? How can they not understand that I need this? Wait, did I do the right thing? Did forgiving him and deciding to love him mean that I needed to ask him to give me away? Did I just reach out to my dad at the expense of hurting my mom? What just happened here? Did my brother really mean that he isn't going to attend the wedding if I let my dad give me away? How did my fairytale turn into a nightmare so fast?*

I finally stepped outside to escape the anger in the room and quickly asked, "God, now what?"

I returned after a few minutes and began to share what I had learned about this amazing concept called *"grace"* and told them they were both right about James not deserving this opportunity. Nevertheless, I continued to share with them that we were all recipients of this same grace, and none of us deserved it. I explained to them that my decision was final, and I would respect and abide by whatever decision they made as a result. "This topic will never be open to discussion with me again." They were still angry, but somehow, I felt better and experienced a peace about my decision.

On the day of the wedding, I was preparing for my entrance because the music to "The Bridal Chorus" would start in 20 minutes. I asked my maid of honor to look for my dad and bring him to the room where we were getting ready. She returned, asking for a description. Although we had been friends for over ten years, she had never seen James. She finally found my mom and asked her to identify my dad. When she returned to my dressing room, I looked at her expectantly. She said, "Sonja, he's not here."

I took a deep breath and asked her to clear the room. I cried. I was so embarrassed. I felt ashamed and foolish for even believing that he would come. I did not have a Plan B; that he would not show up never once crossed my mind. *How could I put myself in this situation? How did I not have a Plan B in place?* Even though he never kept any of his promises, I expected him to be at my wedding. Thoughts continued to race through my mind. I felt like his absence once again impacted my life negatively, and I felt helpless.

I said to myself, "This ruins everything! Now nobody will be talking about how beautiful I look (a tragedy all by itself, in my eyes). Instead they will **ALL** be talking about how my dad stood me up." I could picture everyone's whispering and saying, "What's wrong with her? She couldn't even get her dad to give her away at her wedding."

Surely, this reality existed only in my head. Most of the audience knew nothing of my relationship with my dad, and those who did were not thinking of him at the time. This experience, along with others, demonstrated that pain will take on personalities, voices, and faces that do not really exist but appear very real to the person who feeds them. In this case, I was the one feeding them.

Then I remembered a Scripture or portions of Scriptures well enough to remind me that when my mother and father forsake me, then the Lord would be there for me (Psalm 27:10). I dried my tears and invited some of my wedding party to come back into the room and said, "Let's go." They were sad for me, and several offered to walk down the aisle with me, so I wouldn't be alone. They even suggested some other men who were in the audience as a substitute for my dad.

Bless their hearts. I had a peace that allowed me to say to them, "Ladies, I'm not walking down alone; my FATHER is giving me away. Now go on and get this started; people are waiting to see me in this dress." We laughed, and they exited, leaving me alone for a few minutes. All was well with my soul.

I heard a tap on the door and knew it was time for me to enter. I opened the door and guess who was standing there? My only brother, Bivin, was all dressed up and looking incredibly handsome. We had not spoken in months because of the decision I had made regarding my dad's giving me away. But on this day, this very important day, my brother was waiting for me. He had a serious look on his face as he hugged me.

While we were embracing, he whispered in my ear, "I'm here for you." Speaking of my dad, he added, "It's his loss." When the music to "The Bridal Chorus" began to play, our arms were locked in the escort position, and I felt the love of God flow over me. I *saw* God work in my brother. Bivin smiled and whispered to me again, "Walk slow; this is a new suit." We giggled all the way down the aisle. Nothing else mattered.

Several years passed, and I received a phone call from James' sister to informed me that he had Stage IV lung cancer and was under hospice care. "LaSonja, I think it would be good for him if you came for a visit."

Once I had agreed to make the trip, the Devil didn't wait long to whisper in my other ear, "Now, he wouldn't drive from Houston to Dallas for your wedding, but you are expected to fly from California to Dallas for her brother?" I returned my focus to the phone call, and his sister seemed relieved that I committed to visit.

"I cannot wait to see the look on his face from your surprise visit," she added.

*Surprise? You mean, he didn't initiate this? He's dying, and he didn't ask for me? So, this wasn't even his idea?*

I grabbed my nearest journal and wrote pages and pages; a whole new set of emotions came into play. My mission was to sort, define, and settle them. This was the first personal encounter of someone's dying whom I loved, and I was in a fog. I read several books and read over sermon notes, and thankfully, it helped. I wrote down what seemed like a billion questions for which I needed answers, and I even had a few fill in the blank scripts for James—in case he needed help saying all the things I had pictured him saying all of my life. Some of the questions from my journal included the following:

*Did you think of me on my birthdays?*

*When is my birthday?*

*Did you ever talk to your friends about me?*

*What did you say?*

*Do you remember the only present I ever received from you? What was it?*

*What did you usually do on the holidays?*

*Did you miss me?*

*Do you have any pictures of me?*

*What's your favorite color?*

*Do you have a favorite television show?*

*Do you have a favorite song?*

*Do you have a favorite movie?*

*What are some of the things you wish you could have taught me?*

These few questions do not represent even half of the list, believe me. I left spaces after each question so that I could record his answers. Yes, I planned to interview a dying man because I needed answers. I did not even consider how these questions would impact him; besides, this was the least he could do for me, right? Wrong! When we have unmet needs, we really will go to many lengths to meet them. We remain vulnerable when we do not cast all of our cares (and unmet needs) on the Lord (I Peter 5:7). My focus was totally on *me*, and I was running out of time.

A few weeks passed, and I was sitting at the airport, picturing James making up for 25 years of neglect and thinking about our meeting. *He's going to sit me down and confess his faults and profess his love for me. He's going to express all the sad moments he experienced because he wasn't involved in my life.* I even pictured a stack of birthday cards that he never mailed to me. I had three hours to create this scene, and I used every minute. Yes, I have an overactive imagination, and unfortunately, I still use it as a coping mechanism to escape.

After my long hours of imagining, I was in a car with James' sister, and soon enough, I ring the doorbell. When he answered, he had the biggest smile on his face and hugged me as tight as he could; he didn't say anything—just smiled. Then I noticed his frail body. Although he was excited, he quickly began to walk back to his bedroom with his oxygen tank. I was not prepared for this scene at all. I knew he had lung cancer, but the sister did not warn me about the weight loss or the oxygen tank. His debility was not a part of my plan. He didn't appear strong enough to have the hours of conversations that I had rehearsed in my head.

His sister left the apartment, so we could spend time together. I put my bag down in the living room and returned to his bedside with my journal full of questions. I didn't know how many we would complete in one session, so I wanted to get started right away. As I opened my journal, with pen in hand, I noticed James' eyes were looking at me. *He looks concerned,* I thought.

I explained, "I took some time to write down some questions because I want to know a lot of things about you. I have some questions I want you to answer."

He looked very sad. Then he attempted to speak, but his voice was softer than a whisper, and his speech was impaired. He could not pronounce several letters; therefore, comprehension was nearly impossible. *He's suffering from lung cancer; his inability to speak now made sense.*

I closed my journal and pretended that everything was okay, only it wasn't. I walked outside to cry. I cried for several reasons: one, because I had finally figured out a plan to address my hurts and disappointments, and all he had to do was answer my questions, but he couldn't even do that. I had spent weeks adding to this list of questions, and his answers were supposed to bring healing. I was angry with him. Then I cried because I felt bad for the way I was thinking and feeling. *How can I look for answers from a man on his deathbed? Where is my sensitivity?* I was hurting. I sat in my rental car for hours; after all, I do some of my best thinking in the car.

I felt embarrassed; I felt ashamed; I felt angry; I felt confused; I felt lonely; I felt tired. I tried to think of all the Bible verses that I had memorized and hoped one would stick. I recited Matthew 11:28, which says, *"Come to me, all of you who are weary and burdened, and I will give you rest."* That Scripture contained the invitation I definitely needed. I gave God all my dead hopes and asked Him for my next steps. I really believe God told me to go to sleep. The next morning, I woke up with several Scriptures in my heart and studied them. I wrote in my journal that God did not send me there as James' daughter; I was there as God's daughter and servant. My mission now became clear.

Later that day, I returned to James' bedside and talked to him about Jesus. I told him about the thief on the cross who never attended a Bible study, never paid the tithe, and never prayed until his dying moment. I explained to James that he too could be with Jesus in paradise if he trusted God in this way. He pointed to his closet, and I didn't understand what he was trying to tell me. To understand what he was trying to communicate, I began asking him a series of questions. He continued to shake his head no, and I could see his frustration mounting. I walked toward the closet door to see if I could navigate his directive. Once I figured out that he wanted me to open the closet door, I saw a Bible at the top. He was so weak; the Bible was too heavy for him to hold so he gestured for me to open it.

In the front of the Bible was the letter I had written to him nearly ten years earlier. I asked if he was ready to pray the prayer, and he nodded "yes." We prayed, and James became a Christian on that day.

The next trip I made to visit him, I took both of my sons. While none of my questions were ever answered and I never heard any of the scripts I rehearsed in my head, I learned to acknowledge my unmet needs, meet the needs of others in the meantime (even if it is a struggle), and confess embarrassing thoughts and feelings. Most importantly, I learned the importance of serving God even when I have needs that have not been met. James died about three months later.

Yes, he was my neighbor, and God taught me how to love him.

*Lord, thank You for being the same yesterday, today, and forever. We surrender our hurts, pains, and disappointments to You right now. Remind us to bring our cares to You and allow You to help us to reflect Your love and forgiveness. Remove, with our cooperation, the roots of bitterness that may exist in our hearts today. In Jesus' name, Amen.*

# Operation Meditation

1. List at least three of your favorite love songs. Describe in detail why each one is a favorite. What mood does each song evoke? Why?

2. List at least three favorite Christian songs that talk about love and describe why they are your favorite. What mood does each song evoke? Why?

3. When you think about the Scripture "love your neighbor," what or who immediately comes to your mind?

4. Who is your first memory of pain?

5. How has this pain affected your life?

6. Have you forgiven the person?

7.  Are you willing to forgive the person?

8.  Do you think you can love someone you haven't for-given? If yes, please provide Scripture as your evidence.

9.  What questions do you have for God on this topic? He can handle your questions.

# CHAPTER TWO

# As Thyself

THIS CHAPTER WILL begin differently than the others in this book. I believe your experience will be richer if you will complete the following questions before reading the chapter.

1. Who is the first person you remember who made you feel valued?

2. What did the person do or say to produce that feeling of value within you?

3. What do you see when you look in the mirror? Whose voice do you hear?

4. What did you grow up cherishing about yourself?

5. What did you grow up despising about yourself?

6. On what were you complimented the most?

7. Whose approval did you seek the most?

8. It would have been easier to love myself if ___.

9. What message did you receive about your intellect?

10. What message did you receive about your physical appearance?

11. What happened in your life that caused you to feel as if you are not important?

Mark 12:31, *The second is this: "Love your neighbor as yourself."* There is no commandment greater than these.

Have you ever had a learning experience with God and thought, *Okay, this was so exhausting I deserve a spiritual vacation?* Maybe you have worked tirelessly on a project and waited for your supervisor or family to insist that you take a break. Perhaps you have spent long hours at church and believed that the pastor, choir director, women's ministry leader, usher board president, or somebody should tell you to stay home next Sunday and get some rest. Well, maybe you will be able to relate to my next adventure.

After God taught me a transforming lesson about loving my neighbor, I was ready for a spiritual vacation. I had learned a crucial Christian principle about loving those who did not love me, and now I could relax for a while and celebrate my new level of knowledge. I woke up the next morning to meet God for our scheduled appointment. I reflected in my journal about accepting the people I knew God expected me to love as neighbors and wrote several clarifying questions for God.

I wanted to know if my new commitment to love my neighbors meant that He expected me to be a friend to them, call them on the phone, take them to lunch, sit next to them in church, send them cards, and develop relationships with them. I am very literal; sometimes, I need concrete information in order to meet expectations of others, especially when they don't think like I do. God definitely fits into the category of not thinking like me.

Isaiah 55:8-9, *"For my thoughts are not your thoughts, neither are your ways my ways,"* declares the LORD. *As the heavens are higher than the earth, so are my ways higher than your ways and my thoughts than your thoughts."*

I took a deep breath of relief when this Scripture came to my mind because I realized that God would continue to teach guide me in this area. I didn't have to have all the answers. God wasn't expecting me to figure out how to do His will. He had shared with me that loving my neighbor is a matter of the heart. He was now helping me understand that if my actions are not a result of a heart that is seeking to please Him, I have not accomplished the goal that He set for me. I accepted this perception and began to look forward to beginning the spiritual vacation I felt was due me. I began to peruse the Bible for something light to read; I didn't want to be convicted, persuaded or admonished. I turned to Psalm 23 because the passage makes me happy; however, God re-directed me to Mark 12:31. This time, my eyes were focused on the last part of the verse: *As thyself.* I stared at the two words, feeling as if God was dragging His feet and delaying my Bible break.

I began reading the two words aloud. Then I declared, "I love me! I must be reading the wrong thing." However, I could hear the uncertainty in my voice, so I said it again—louder. There was a strange silence in the room; the declaration of my love for me quickly became a question. "Lord, I love me, right?"

It was if God said, "Do you?"

I knew I was in trouble because God never asks questions to which He needs the answer. After all, He knows everything. *That question is for me!* Suddenly, I felt like the rewind button on my life had been pressed. The scenes were full of decisions I had made while trying to please other people, roles I had decided to play even when I knew better, actions that had placed the value of others above my own, sacrifices I had made while secretly resenting the receiver, things for which I had taken responsibility that were not my fault, and things I had accepted that were not in my best interest. Tears flooded my eyes and began to pour from a fountain that appeared to have no knob to turn them off.

I remember David's pouring his heart out to God when Saul was trying to kill him; in Psalm 56:8 (NLT) he expressed, *"You keep track of all my sorrows. You have collected all of my tears in your bottle. You have recorded each one in your book."* I felt only His love—no judgment. While God knew that I didn't really love myself, I knew I needed to acknowledge it. God, in His compassionate way, began to teach me through His Word that I needed to allow His view of me to penetrate my heart in such a way that it would change the way I saw myself. In order to love myself, I needed to see my value. I began at the cross and ended at the empty tomb. John 3:16 (KJV), *"For God so loved the world* [including me], *that He gave His only begotten Son, that whosoever believeth in him should not perish, but have everlasting life."*

Identity, self-worth, self-esteem, and value are all abstract concepts for many people. One definition given for the word *identity* is "who you are, the way you think about yourself, the way you are viewed by the world, and the characteristics that define you." The world defines you by your profession and your possessions. In other words, you are defined by where you work, where you live, what you drive, and what you wear. If you are not careful, you will use the same criteria to define yourself and others.

Why is it that when you meet someone, one of the first questions you ask is "What do you do for a living?" Is it because you think you can ascertain important information about a person from the answer to this question? What people do for a living

*What people do for a living or their professions oftentimes has very little to do with WHO they are.*

or their professions oftentimes has very little to do with WHO they are. You may gain an idea of how much money they make or their ranking in an organization, but this information is shallow. How often do you find yourself saying, "I should be further along than this? I should have more than this?" On what are these questions based? Who or what is your reference point?

The world constantly creates categories for people. Take the rental car and airline industry. If you spend a certain amount of money with them, they will give you a priority status of silver, gold, or platinum; this status comes with perks. Unfortunately, this categorization of people even happens in some churches. Depending on who you are, you may receive preferential seating and treatment. If you give a certain dollar amount, your donation may be announced publicly and even labeled as a "special offering." Who has the right to label an offering as "special"?

Psalm 139:2 says that only God knows the heart. Jesus acknowledged the woman who gave two very small coins. Why? Because she was poor and gave all that she had. Jesus knew her heart (Mark 12:41-44). If God has blessed you financially and has allowed you the experience of first-class or platinum membership, great! Just know that this is not WHO you are; it's access you have been granted by God. He is your source. Deuteronomy 8:18 says, *"But remember the LORD your God, for it is he who gives you the ability to produce wealth....*" God alone gives the power to gain wealth.

On that same note, if you are on the opposite side of this scenario and you sit in the coach section of the plane and do not see your name in lights when renting a car, be encouraged because this is not a reflection of WHO you are. Resist the temptation to measure your worth by this materialistic system.

I worked with a teacher (who became a dear friend) named K. Rodriguez. Before she administered tests to her students, she would make the same announcement: "This test is a reflection of what you know—NOT who you are." She was keenly aware of how students equate their grades with their personal worth and identities. She was intentional in addressing this reality.

*"As thyself."* Who are you? If you are to love your neighbor as yourself, you must identify who you really are. How do you demonstrate this self-love? What standards are you using? We live in a world that uses a variety of superficial criteria to assign value to people. A value is placed on people who eat meat, on people who do not, on people who work blue-collar jobs, on women who have children and on women who do not, on people who attend small churches, on people who attend megachurches, on male pastors who lead churches, on females who pastor churches, and this list could go on.

*Some of the things we have acquired really were not for us; they were for the applause of others.*

If we are honest with ourselves, we would admit that we also use material criteria to define us. Some of the things we have acquired really were not for us; they were for the applause of others. Trying to gain the approval of others is a constant, never-ending job. However, we are driven to send a specific message about ourselves whether or not we believe it. Sometimes, it's what we know about ourselves that drive us to portray something very different.

God wants to deliver us from this act of futility and heal. Romans 5:8 says, *"But God demonstrates his own love for us in this: while we were still sinners, Christ died for us."* This verse means that, at our worst, God had a reason to give us His all. What He knows about you is what really matters.

**Psalm 139:1-16** (NKJV)
*O LORD, you have searched me and known me.*

*2You know my sitting down and my rising up; You understand my thought afar off.*

*3You comprehend my path and my lying down, and are acquainted with all my ways.*

*4For there is not a word on my tongue, but behold, O LORD, You know it altogether.*

*5You have hedged me behind and before and laid your hand upon me.*

*6Such knowledge is too wonderful for me; It is high, I cannot attain it.*

*7Where can I go from your Spirit? Or where can I flee from your presence?*

*8If I ascend into heaven, You are there; If I make my bed in hell, behold, you are there.*

*⁹If I take the wings of the morning, and dwell in the uttermost parts of the sea,*

*¹⁰Even there your hand shall hold me, And Your right hand shall hold me.*

*¹¹If I say, "Surely the darkness shall fall on me," even the night shall be light about me;*

*¹²Indeed, the darkness shall not hide from you, but the night shines as the day; The darkness and the light are both alike to you.*

*¹³For you formed my inwards parts; you covered me in my mother's womb.*

*¹⁴I will praise you, for I am fearfully and wonderfully made; marvelous are your works, and that my soul knows well.*

*¹⁵My frame was not hidden from you, when I was made in secret, and skillfully wrought in the lowest parts of the earth.*

*¹⁶Your eyes saw my substance, being yet unformed. And in your book they all were written, The days fashioned for me, when as yet there were none of them.*

David expressed in Psalm 139 how personally involved God is with each of us. His involvement didn't begin when we accepted Christ. No! It began long before that. He has known and loved us for eternity. Think about that. Before your conception, He already knew you; He had already put you together.

Some of the things that we don't like about ourselves are genetically predetermined. Our eye color, hair texture, height, cup size, and skin complexion were all given at birth. However, most of the things listed can now be altered for a fee. If you can afford to safely alter them, that choice is between you and God. Just remember that God did not make the BMI chart, so He doesn't have a numerical target weight for you. We have set standards for ourselves and oftentimes feel the effects of not measuring up. Our reference points are usually other people we see and sometimes know. God loves you, and indeed, He wants your body to be healthy; after all, He lives there, remember?

Past rejections can make it difficult to be transparent with God. Some of you have been in relationships that appeared to change or end when the other person really got to know the real you. Well, that will never happen with God. As you read in Psalm 139, He knows you and still calls you His own. You can safely come out of hiding; God knows you are tired of running from your past, your insecurities, and Him. He wants us to love ourselves because He does. Remember, we have been declared right because of the finished work of Jesus Christ. Understanding, accepting, and believing God's Word will create a healthy sense of self-esteem. Yes, self-esteem. When we know our God-status, His deity will overshadow your faults.

**Psalm 8:1-8**

*Lord, our Lord, how majestic is your name in all the earth! You have set your glory in the heavens.*

*²Through the praise of children and infants you have established a stronghold against your enemies, to silence the foe and the avenger.*

*3When I consider your heavens, the work of your fingers, the moon and the stars, which you have set in place,*

*4what is mankind that you are mindful of them, human beings that you care for them?*

*5You have made them a little lower than the angels and crowned them with glory and honor.*

*6You made them rulers over the works of your hands; you put everything under their feet:*

*7all flocks and herds, and the animals of the wild,*

*8the birds in the sky, and the fish in the sea, all that swim the paths of the seas.*

God's love for us is amazing! God's love confused David too. David looked at all of the work of his Heavenly Father's hand and how beautiful and perfect everything was, and he was baffled that God had entrusted it all to us. God made us a little lower than the angels, yet the angels cannot sing about redemption. You are loved by God. Love God. Love yourself. Love your neighbor.

*Father, help us to unveil before You; help us to remove all pretense right now. Lord, You know us and love us anyway. I pray that we will become more genuine when we enter Your presence and that this consistent practice with You will enable us to accept ourselves and live transformed and transparent lives before others. In Jesus' name, I pray. Amen.*

# Operation Meditation

According to the Scriptures in this lesson, list several Biblical reasons to love yourself.

# CHAPTER THREE

# I've Given Up Hope

AFTER TEN YEARS of dating the same young man and a 15-year marriage that ended in divorce, I decided I would never get married again. For me, marriage involved more pain than joy, more downs than ups, and way more tears than laughter. During this marriage I learned that only in math do two halves make a whole. When friends talked to me about dating or wanted to introduce me to someone, I quickly stated, "My intention is not to be in a serious relationship. If the other party is looking for something permanent that resembles a commitment, I am not interested."

*During this marriage I learned that only in math do two halves make a whole.*

As time passed, I realized that a part of me desired to be in a committed relationship, but the thought of a marriage and the pain I had experienced in my previous one paralyzed me. I could not imagine a marriage that would not feel like the last one. As a result, I decided one day that marriage wasn't for me because I did not want to experience the agony of hope. Hoping for something different was scary and sometimes felt foolish. Imagining sharing my life with another man and allowing him to know me at my weakest, sharing my vulnerabilities, and trusting that he would care about my feelings was overwhelming, to say the least. This roller coaster of emotions from the discussions with friends was too much for me. I needed to have a funeral for that hope in order to move on with my life. I did not want to hope again.

### The Shunammite's Son Restored to Life
### II Kings 4:8-36

*One day Elisha went to Shunem. And a well-to-do woman was there, who urged him to stay for a meal. So whenever he came by, he stopped there to eat. ⁹She said to her husband, "I know that this man who often comes our way is a holy man of God. ¹⁰Let's make a small room on the roof and put in it a bed and a table, a chair and a lamp for him. Then he can stay there whenever he comes to us."*

*¹¹One day when Elisha came, he went up to his room and lay down there. ¹²He said to his servant Gehazi, "Call the Shunammite." So he called her, and she stood before him. ¹³Elisha said to him, "Tell her, 'You have gone to all this trouble for us. Now what can be done for you? Can we speak on your behalf to the king or the commander of the army?'"*

*She replied, "I have a home among my own people."*

*¹⁴"What can be done for her?" Elisha asked.*

*Gehazi said, "She has no son, and her husband is old."*

*¹⁵Then Elisha said, "Call her." So he called her, and she stood in the doorway. ¹⁶"About this time next year," Elisha said, "you will hold a son in your arms."*

*"No, my lord!" she objected. "Please, man of God, don't mislead your servant!"*

*<sup>17</sup>But the woman became pregnant, and the next year about that same time she gave birth to a son, just as Elisha had told her.*

*<sup>18</sup>The child grew, and one day he went out to his father, who was with the reapers. <sup>19</sup>He said to his father, "My head! My head!"*

*His father told a servant, "Carry him to his mother." <sup>20</sup>After the servant had lifted him up and carried him to his mother, the boy sat on her lap until noon, and then he died. <sup>21</sup>She went up and laid him on the bed of the man of God, then shut the door and went out.*

*<sup>22</sup>She called her husband and said, "Please send me one of the servants and a donkey so I can go to the man of God quickly and return."*

*<sup>23</sup>"Why go to him today?" he asked. "It's not the New Moon or the Sabbath."*

*"That's all right," she said.*

*<sup>24</sup>She saddled the donkey and said to her servant, "Lead on; don't slow down for me unless I tell you." <sup>25</sup>So she set out and came to the man of God at Mount Carmel.*

*When he saw her in the distance, the man of God said to his servant Gehazi, "Look! There's the Shunammite! <sup>26</sup>Run to meet her and ask her, 'Are you all right? Is your husband all right? Is your child all right?'"*

*"Everything is all right," she said.*

*<sup>27</sup>When she reached the man of God at the mountain,*

*she took hold of his feet. Gehazi came over to push her away, but the man of God said, "Leave her alone! She is in bitter distress, but the Lord has hidden it from me and has not told me why."*

*28 "Did I ask you for a son, my lord?" she said. "Didn't I tell you, 'Don't raise my hopes'?"*

*29 Elisha said to Gehazi, "Tuck your cloak into your belt, take my staff in your hand and run. Don't greet anyone you meet, and if anyone greets you, do not answer. Lay my staff on the boy's face."*

*30 But the child's mother said, "As surely as the Lord lives and as you live, I will not leave you." So he got up and followed her.*

*31 Gehazi went on ahead and laid the staff on the boy's face, but there was no sound or response. So Gehazi went back to meet Elisha and told him, "The boy has not awakened."*

*32 When Elisha reached the house, there was the boy lying dead on his couch. 33 He went in, shut the door on the two of them and prayed to the Lord. 34 Then he got on the bed and lay on the boy, mouth to mouth, eyes to eyes, hands to hands. As he stretched himself out on him, the boy's body grew warm. 35 Elisha turned away and walked back and forth in the room and then got on the bed and stretched out on him once more. The boy sneezed seven times and opened his eyes. 36 Elisha summoned Gehazi and said, "Call the Shunammite." And he did. When she came, he said, "Take your son."*

In this passage, we meet a wealthy woman who has a love for God. When the prophet Elisha was in town, she cooked for him, and one day suggested to her husband that they build a room for him. She did not tell her husband what her plans were; she used the words "Let us." This suggestion was a proposal; clearly, she had a vision for this room because she told her husband what she wanted to put in it. However, her husband was definitely an important part of this process.

The next time Elisha came to town and saw the room that had been built for him, he wanted to express his appreciation to the woman. Elisha directed his servant to ask the woman how could he repay her for the hospitality. First, he asked how could he use his influence with the king on her behalf. Then he offered to speak to the captain of the army and give her male family members a distinct place in the army. She responded by saying that she did not have a need. She said she was content; she lived around family members and that was all she needed. She walked away. Living among relatives then oftentimes symbolized support and stability.

Elisha was not satisfied with her answer; he wanted to give her something back. I will not pass up this opportunity to remind us that sometimes the gifts we receive should initiate a genuine desire to give back. *Let's not be consistent receivers.* Elisha probes his servant more and asks, "What can we do for this woman?"

The servant noted, "Well, she doesn't have a son, and her husband is old."

I can imagine Elisha's getting excited about changing this

woman's life with a son. Every Israelite woman wanted a son. Being barren was considered a personal tragedy. A son, especially a firstborn son, was insurance for the mother; he was expected to carry out significant duties. An added benefit to blessing this woman with a son was that her husband was aging; the possibilities of her becoming a widow must have been close.

I can hear Elisha's telling the Shunammite the good news. "Woman, I have great news for you. This time next year, you will have a son."

Only the Shunammite woman was not happy. Her response is proof. She said, "No, please don't play with my emotions. I have already accepted the fact that I cannot have children; it is what it is. I don't want to hope again."

But God knew that having a baby was a real desire at one point that had not gone away; she had learned how to live with the pain. God, being God, did exactly what He said. He gave her a son.

As you read in the text, the son became sick one day, and the Shunammite mother held him on her lap for hours until he died. Can you imagine the thoughts going through her mind? The Bible doesn't tell us her thoughts, but a couple of mine include the following:

- "I didn't ask for this."
- "This is why I told him to leave well enough alone."

You probably have some thoughts of your own. Look at the response of the woman when her son died. She took the time to take him upstairs and place him on Elisha's bed. She did not panic. She decided to go to the prophet. On her way out, her husband said, "It's not Sunday or Wednesday night Bible study. Why are going to see the prophet?"

She told him where she was going but did not mention why. Her disposition could not have been distraught, or he would have known why. Her eyes must not have been puffy from crying; surely he would have known something was wrong. She never told him that their son was dead. This woman was deeply wounded, but she knew where to go: to the prophet, God's representative.

Thank God for Jesus, now we can go to Him directly. We must note that even when a gift comes from God, it may not be affliction-free. She was a recipient of a miracle; she knew firsthand that God can do the impossible. Armed with this knowledge, she went to see the man of God. Once she reached him, she first placed herself in a position of humility. She also reminded Elisha that she did not want to hope again.

I can imagine her saying, "With all due respect, sir, I told you not to get my hopes up. I was living with the pain of never having a child, and that was better than this pain of losing one."

Elisha knew the Shunammite woman was in bitter distress. God can handle our frustrations and our disappointments, even our attitudes—if we stay in His presence long enough to hear Him speak. God should always have the last word.

*God should always have the last word.*

Elisha sent his servant to the woman's house, but she told Elisha that she would not leave him. But wait, she had told her husband that she would return. This kind of faith sounds like the faith that Abraham possessed when he said, *"Wait here, the lad and I will return"* (Genesis 22:5).

Once Elisha prayed and God returned life into the Shunnamite's son, he told the servant to call for the woman. The fact that she had to be called means she wasn't waiting by the door or around the corner. She trusted the man of God and walked away from the situation. The Bible said that the boy sneezed seven times. If she had heard him sneeze, she still determined to maintain her disposition of waiting and trusting. If she didn't hear him sneeze, she still maintained a distance that would keep her from interfering or being tempted to get involved.

I have had people express to me that their belief about prayer is that once you pray to God about a matter, your faith should cause you never to bring it up again. I do not accept that belief because it is not aligned with the truth of God's Word. Matthew 7:7-8 instructs the believer to ask, seek, and knock. Luke 18:1-5 spotlights the parable about the persistent widow, who did not stop asking. Paul prayed three times about the same matter, asking God for deliverance (2 Corinthians 12:7-9).

The Shunammite woman demonstrates faith in action. She has done everything in her power to address her situation, and she sees God's involvement. She was far enough not to hear or respond to his sneezing, yet close enough to hear her name called to receive her answer. She totally trusted God with the process.

Would you admit that you would have been in the room on

the first sneeze with a box of tissue, a blanket, soup and orange juice? Of course, your presence would have been in case God needed your help.

There was a time in my life that I know as soon as the prophet would have opened the door to tell his servant to call for me, I would have fallen into the room! I would have been leaning on the door. Not this woman! She's modeling trust in God for us. God doesn't even give her a name, but He gives her a place in the Bible.

Once the servant called the woman, she responded by walking—not running—into the room. Elisha told her to take her son. She did not. Instead, she fell at his feet again and bowed to the ground. She worshipped first and then took her son. As happy as she must have been, she took the time to worship and thank the man of God. God is glorified when we decide to take our wounds to Him and remain in a position of humility throughout the process.

*Lord, thank You for each gift You have given me, the relationships You have restored, and the hope You have renewed. Please forgive me for not trusting You with the situations You are pointing out to me right now. As I commit to a deeper study of Your Word, help me to apply it to my life in a way that is pleasing to You. You care so much for women that You have taken the time to use the relationship between a mother and a child to demonstrate to me that no relationship should ever take precedence over the one I am seeking to build with*

———

*You. You showed us Your love for her, her love for her son and how keeping You first brings healing. Lord, I have watched some things die. Heal me, please. Help me to bring all of my cares to You because You care about me and trust the outcome to You—whether it's a resurrection or a benediction. Lord, humility isn't popular, and I don't even hear the word much, but teach me what being humble looks like to You. In the redeeming name of Jesus, I pray. Amen.*

———

# Operation Meditation

1. Think of a situation you encountered that did not end the way you wanted it to end. What was your response to God?

2. The woman created a space for Elisha in her home. Do you have a space in your home where you meet God? If not, can you picture a place you can designate for this purpose?

3. What have you decided to live without because you have given up hope?

4. What are you living with because it's too painful to hope again?

# CHAPTER FOUR

# Pride Aside

ABOUT 25 YEARS AGO, God taught me several lessons the hard way. Let me give you the background of one of them; if I listed them all, this book would never end.

A man whom I will call Chester attended the same church that I did. I did not like Chester because he was manipulative, deceptive, and unfaithful to his wife. He and the man to whom I was married for 15 years spent a lot of time together and shared this "unfaithful" title. Frankly, I blamed Chester for some of the decisions my former husband made. Blaming Chester was easier than believing he voluntarily left his wife and children at home while he slept with other women. Needless to say, whenever I saw Chester, I was neither Christian nor cordial. In fact, I openly displayed my disgust for him. I didn't ever want anyone to say that I was a pretender—well, at least not in this area.

One night, I was driving on a busy street in Los Angeles with my one-year-old son and noticed that the car was not accelerating properly. I began to check the dashboard to see if any warning lights were flashing, and to my surprise, the gas gauge was registering below the "E" for empty. This happened before cell phones were commonplace, and I didn't know what I was going to do. I was afraid to get out of my car and present the vulnerable picture of a lost 23-year-old with a baby in her arms. I sat in the car for what felt like hours but was actually about 30 minutes.

Then a car pulled up next to mine, and I heard a voice call my name and ask, "Do you need some help?"

To my chagrin, I saw that Chester was the one offering his help. Believe it or not, I actually entertained the idea of saying, "No, thanks." He was the last person I wanted to need. I was angry with God for not sending someone else; I was also embarrassed because of all the strong, negative feelings I had about this man.

*God is sometimes orchestrating these embarrassing and helpless incidents to teach us to put aside our pride.*

God taught me several pertinent lessons on this night, and the one I will share with you is, as Christians, God is sometimes orchestrating these embarrassing and helpless incidents to teach us to put aside our pride.

### 2 Kings 4:1-7

*The wife of a man from the company of the prophets cried out to Elisha, "Your servant my husband is dead, and you know that he revered the Lord. But now his creditor is coming to take my two boys as his slaves."*

*²Elisha replied to her, "How can I help you? Tell me, what do you have in your house?"*

*"Your servant has nothing there at all," she said, "except a small jar of olive oil."*

*³Elisha said, "Go around and ask all your neighbors*

*for empty jars. Don't ask for just a few. ⁴Then go inside and shut the door behind you and your sons. Pour oil into all the jars, and as each is filled, put it to one side."*

*⁵She left him and shut the door behind her and her sons. They brought the jars to her and she kept pouring. ⁶When all the jars were full, she said to her son, "Bring me another one."*

*But he replied, "There is not a jar left." Then the oil stopped flowing.*

*⁷She went and told the man of God, and he said, "Go, sell the oil and pay your debts. You and your sons can live on what is left."*

This passage is a snapshot of the widow of a prophet who cries out to Elisha about her situation. She has creditors threatening to take her sons to pay her husband's debt. She did not call her husband names for leaving her in this dire predicament; neither does she say anything negative about him. She was seeking God for assistance with her dilemma.

When I read Elisha's response, I chuckle because I can just imagine my own response to his response. "How can you help me? Are you serious? I just told you that I need money because they are going to take my sons as slaves."

Elisha also asked the widow what she had in her house. He was asking her to do a quick inventory of what she had in her possession. Her immediate response was, "I don't have anything."

Have you ever sent your child to a room to look for something, and the child returns so quickly you know he or she did not really look? That's the picture I have of this conversation.

The widow's first response was "I don't have anything." It's easy to minimize what you have when what you need is so much more. But she does add, *"except a little oil."* Your little *without* God is frustrating and depressing, but your little *with* God does a miracle make. Consider these passages where God only needed a little to make a miracle.

## The Five Loaves and Two Fishes
### Matthew 14:14-21

*When Jesus landed and saw a large crowd, he had compassion on them and healed their sick. [15]As evening approached, the disciples came to him and said, "This is a remote place, and it's already getting late. Send the crowds away, so they can go to the villages and buy themselves some food."*

*[16]Jesus replied, "They do not need to go away. You give them something to eat."*

*[17]"We have here only five loaves of bread and two fish," they answered.*

*[18]"Bring them here to me," he said. And he directed the people to sit down on the grass. Taking the five loaves and the two fish and looking up to heaven, he gave thanks and broke the loaves. Then he gave them to the disciples, and the disciples gave them to the people. They all ate and were satisfied, and the disciples picked up twelve basketfuls of broken pieces that were left over. The*

number of those who ate was about five thousand men, besides women and children.

## The Widow at Zarephath
### I Kings 17:10-16

So he [Elijah] went to Zarephath. When he came to the town gate, a widow was there gathering sticks. He called to her and asked, "Would you bring me a little water in a jar so I may have a drink?" <sup>11</sup>As she was going to get it, he called, "And bring me, please, a piece of bread."

<sup>12</sup>"As surely as the LORD your God lives," she replied, "I don't have any bread—only a handful of flour in a jar and a little olive oil in a jug. I am gathering a few sticks to take home and make a meal for myself and my son, that we may eat it—and die."

<sup>13</sup>Elijah said to her, "Don't be afraid. Go home and do as you have said. But first make a small loaf of bread for me from what you have and bring it to me, and then make something for yourself and your son. <sup>14</sup>For this is what the LORD, the God of Israel, says: 'The jar of flour will not be used up and the jug of oil will not run dry until the day the Lord sends rain on the land.'"

<sup>15</sup>She went away and did as Elijah had told her. So there was food every day for Elijah and for the woman and her family. For the jar of flour was not used up and the jug of oil did not run dry, in keeping with the word of the LORD spoken by Elijah.

## David and Goliath
### I Samuel 17:45-50

*David said to the Philistine, "You come against me with sword and spear and javelin, but I come against you in the name of the* LORD *Almighty, the God of the armies of Israel, whom you have defied.* <sup>46</sup>*This day the* LORD *will deliver you into my hands, and I'll strike you down and cut off your head. This very day I will give the carcasses of the Philistine army to the birds and the wild animals, and the whole world will know that there is a God in Israel.* <sup>47</sup>*All those gathered here will know that it is not by sword or spear that the* LORD *saves; for the battle is the* LORD*'s, and he will give all of you into our hands."*

<sup>48</sup>*As the Philistine moved closer to attack him, David ran quickly toward the battle line to meet him.* <sup>49</sup>*Reaching into his bag and taking out a stone, he slung it and struck the Philistine on the forehead. The stone sank into his forehead, and he fell facedown on the ground.*

<sup>50</sup>*So David triumphed over the Philistine with a sling and a stone; without a sword in his hand he struck down the Philistine and killed him.*

God can do a lot when we acknowledge our lack and surrender our "little."

Elisha gave the widow clear instructions. "Go and ask." "Go inside and shut the door behind you." He tells her to go to all her neighbors for empty jars. *All? Really? Even the Chesters?* Surely people already knew her situation, and now she must ask for help. Not only did she have to go to *all* the neighbors, she had to ask for more than a few.

Asking required humility on her part; after all, she was a woman. If we women have a hard time telling God we need something from Him, imagine the widow having to ask her neighbors; it had to be harder. Think about her situation. One day she was married to a prophet; the next day she was begging for jars her neighbors weren't using. What if she would have decided to try to find another prophet to give her a solution that she liked? Undoubtedly, she would have missed her blessing. God is not in the business of doing for us what we can do for ourselves. He requires teamwork; He is not an enabling Father.

Elisha told her to go inside. God wants to do some things for us in private; sometimes it's a family affair. She was told to shut the door. God wants some miracles to happen behind closed doors; sometimes, people aren't allowed to see your miracle taking place. They have to wait for you to tell them about it. But like the woman at the well, when you are the only one there, make sure you tell others what God has done for you. I found it interesting that the woman says nothing else after Elisha gave her directions. She didn't even ask him what to do once all the jars were filled. Her immediate obedience is exemplary. Once her son told her that there were no more empty jars, the oil stopped flowing. Elisha put her to work; she put her sons to work. They were evidently old enough to

*God never runs out of anything; we simply stop taking our empty vessels to Him.*

be sold as slaves, so they were able to physically help with part of the task. Not only did they partner with their mom in an obedient act, but they were also given an opportunity to be participants in a miracle. As long as there were empty vessels, there was oil to pour. God never runs out of anything; we simply stop taking our empty vessels to Him.

Once her mission was completed, she went to the prophet for her next step. He gave her a plan that would sustain her, "You and your sons can live on what's left."

# Operation Meditation

1. What is God telling you to do that will require you to put aside your pride?

2. When was the last time you shared how God met your needs with your children?

3. Are you in a predicament that was caused by someone else? If so, have you taken it to God? What plan has He given you? Have you put His answer in place?

# CHAPTER FIVE

# Nobody Likes Today

**Matthew 6:25-34**

*"Therefore I tell you, do not worry about your life, what you will eat or drink; or about your body, what you will wear. Is not life more than food, and the body more than clothes? [26]Look at the birds of the air; they do not sow or reap or store away in barns, and yet your heavenly Father feeds them. Are you not much more valuable than they? [27]Can any one of you by worrying add a single hour to your life?*

*[28]"And why do you worry about clothes? See how the flowers of the field grow. They do not labor or spin. [29]Yet I tell you that not even Solomon in all his splendor was dressed like one of these. [30]If that is how God clothes the grass of the field, which is here today and tomorrow is thrown into the fire, will he not much more clothe you— you of little faith? [31]So do not worry, saying, 'What shall we eat?' or 'What shall we drink?' or 'What shall we wear?' [32]For the pagans run after all these things, and your heavenly Father knows that you need them. [33]But seek first his kingdom and his righteousness, and all these things will be given to you as well. [34]Therefore do not worry about tomorrow, for tomorrow will worry about itself. Each day has enough trouble of its own.*

---

I WELL REMEMBER expecting my first son nearly 27 years ago! I couldn't wait to feel him move, then I couldn't wait to deliver him, then I couldn't wait see him, then I couldn't wait for him to go to sleep, then I couldn't wait for him to sleep through the night, then I couldn't wait for him to crawl, then walk, and then talk (I was quick to regret this one). Before I knew it, he was his own little person. I also remember watching him climb into his bed and asking God, "Where did all the time go?"

I felt as if God again pressed the rewind button of my mind. I heard my voice say over and over, "I can't wait until this… I can't wait until that…." None of what I was waiting for was going to happen on the current day. Tears began to run down my face, and I said aloud, "I have wished away two years of my son's life. I didn't enjoy the entire growth process because I was focused on the milestones. I couldn't enjoy the milestones because I quickly focused on the next one. That time was lost; I can never get it back.

*I couldn't enjoy the milestones because I quickly focused on the next one.*

Have you listened to yourself lately? Does this scenario sound familiar? Do you hear yourself saying any the following comments? "I can't wait until Friday." "I can't wait until payday." "I can't wait until Thanksgiving." "I can't wait until Christmas." "I can't wait for the holidays to be over." "I can't wait until vacation." "I can't wait to get back home and sleep in my own bed." "I can't wait for my kids to go back to school." "I can't wait for my kids to graduate and move out." "I can't wait for my kids to come visit." "I can't wait for that dream job." "I can't wait to get a new car." "I can't wait to pay off this car." The comments are endless.

For years, my niece has talked about getting married; she has often voiced her desire to experience all that engagement has to offer. Last year, she got engaged. I called her one day to share in the excitement, and I lost count of the number of times I heard her say, "I'm just ready for this to be over! I'm over all this wedding stuff."

Nobody seems to like today. We often quote Psalm 118:24 (KJV), which says, *"This is the day which the LORD hath made, we will rejoice and be glad in it,"* but we don't live like it. We cannot enjoy today if we are pressing fast forward to get to tomorrow. Many of us have missed some important moments and missions because we were focused on tomorrow, next week, next month, and even next year. In the passage that began this chapter, Jesus shared the do's and do not's of how to live life (Matthew 6:25-43). Worrying about tomorrow won't add anything to our life. This truth even applies if we are excitedly waiting on something positive.

> *"Be anxious for nothing, but in everything by prayer and supplication, with thanksgiving, let your requests be made known to God"* (Philippians 4:6).

We know this Scripture and principle, but we do not apply it. Research states that few things shorten life more than worry.

When you see the word *"therefore"* in Scripture, look ahead to see what the word is referring to. In Matthew 6:25-43, after *"therefore,"* God lists our worries. Jesus knows these things will happen. But we can rest assured that Jesus is already in tomorrow; He has an answer for each question and solutions for each problem.

*The way has been made; God isn't still working on anything.* Please note that God is not making a way for your problems nor is He working on your problems. It is finished. The way has been made; God isn't still working on anything. He reveals in His own time. God is in the past, present, and future. Our minds are too finite to comprehend this concept, so don't try! Faith comes in when our finite minds can't. We chose to believe—even when it surpasses our understanding.

Second Peter 3:8 says that with the Lord, a thousand years is but a day and a day is but a thousand years. Then God tells us that He knows the exact number of hairs on our head. We lose strands every day, but He never loses track. He's God; that's just the way God operates. Nobody knows you like God does, and every day is a gift that He wants you to enjoy.

Lamentations 3:22-23 says, *"Because of the LORD's great love we are not consumed, for his compassions never fail. They are new every morning; great is your faithfulness."* The thief on the cross asked Jesus to remember him when He came into His kingdom. Jesus could have easily said, "Next week you will be with Me," but He didn't. Jesus said, "**Today** you will be with Me in paradise."

———

*Lord, thank You for our daily bread, thank You for mercy that is new everyday, and thank You for giving us a new perspective on the daily gift of life. Help us to redefine our priorities and trust You for daily provisions, as You desire. Help us to enjoy and live in the now. Forgive us for rushing through days as if tomorrow will have more value. In Jesus' name I pray, Amen.*

———

# Operation Meditation

1. What are you worried about right now?

2. How often does worry interrupt your days?

3. How many times has God failed you?

4. Have you fallen into the trap of trying to get ahead of God and solve your own future problems?

5. What immediate need in your life are you neglecting because you are worried about the future?

6. If God told you how and when He was going to meet every need you have for the next year, how would you spend your days?

7. How often do you think you would start thinking about the year after that? Be honest.

8. How can you start to trust God for your daily bread?

# CHAPTER SIX

# Spiritual Warfare

W HEN I WAS growing up, I occasionally attended church with some family members. The teaching of this church required women to wear long sleeves (even in the summer), no jewelry but wedding rings, no pants, and no makeup. No secular music was allowed. This reference is not to make a mockery of their religion; however, all of these do not's translated to me as NO FUN. I was 13 and not only did I decide never to return to that church, but I also felt that I could never please a God like that. I was angry at God and wrote in my diary, "Who would want to serve a God with all these rules?" The picture of God I had in my mind was more like a mean Judge in the sky. Then I wrote a resolve: "I will just get saved when I am old; I want to have fun, and God is against this."

One day when I was talking to my cousin, Avita, I informed her that I had decided to accept Christ as my personal Savior a few weeks earlier. She volunteered to come to my house for a personal Bible study to address some of the questions I had about God and all of His rules. We studied Exodus 32:1-35 and 34:1-9. These passages talk about Aaron and the children of Israel taking off their jewelry and making an idol. Avita mentioned that these could possibly be the Scriptures taken out of context and used as confirmation that women should not wear jewelry.

I felt better after hearing her explanation—not that I had jewelry to wear, but I knew I wanted to buy some one day. The main rule I was concerned about was this "no-pants" issue. My wardrobe consisted of pants only. That's all I had. I had to borrow dresses when I went to church. We also studied Deuteronomy 22:5 (KJV) which states, *"The woman shall not wear that which pertaineth unto a man, neither shall a man put on a woman's garment…."* My cousin quickly pointed out to me that when this was written, men were not wearing pants; therefore, this Scripture was also being taken out of context when used as a basis to forbid women from wearing pants. She spent several hours sharing God's Word with me. I gained a Biblical understanding of the God I thought was so mean. Before my cousin left, she adamantly shared the importance of developing a habit of studying God's Word on a regular basis. I committed. Yes, the topic is Spiritual Warfare.

On a Wednesday night in 1989, the Bible study lesson was on **Ephesians 6:10-18:**

*Finally, be strong in the Lord and in his might power. [11]Put on the full armor of God, so that you can take your stand against the devil's schemes. [12]For our struggle is not against flesh and blood, but against the rulers, against the authorities, against the powers of this dark world and against the spiritual forces of evil in the heavenly realms. [13]Therefore put on the whole armor of God, so that when the day of evil comes, you may be able to stand your ground, and after you have done everything, to stand.*

*¹⁴Stand firm then, with the belt of truth buckled around your waist, with the breastplate of righteousness in place, ¹⁵and with your feet fitted with the readiness that comes from the gospel of peace. ¹⁶In addition to all this, take up the shield of faith, with which you can extinguish all the flaming arrows of the evil one. ¹⁷Take the helmet of salvation and the sword of the Spirit, which is the word of God.*

*¹⁸And pray in the Spirit on all occasions with all kinds of prayers and requests. With this in mind, be alert and always keep on praying for all the Lord's people.*

I had a 40-minute drive home from my church, and I continued to think about the lesson and listen to my Christian music cassettes. The next day I was ready to practice what I had learned. When I entered my mother's house, I noticed my mom and one of my sisters standing in the kitchen. My sister was loud and angry. When I came closer, I saw that she was holding a knife to my mom's throat.

Mom yelled, "Leave the house!" but two Scriptures flashed quickly to my mind and spirit: *"We wrestle not against flesh and blood..."* and I John 4:4, which says, *"Ye are of God, little children, and have overcome them: because greater is he that is in you, than he that is in the world."*

I took the knife from my sister, put her out of the house, and spent time sitting on my bed trying to figure out what had just happened. God used my time in Bible study to prepare me for this encounter. I was excited about going to bed and waking up the next day to implement my new learning, but God knew that my battle was a lot closer than the next day. I must confess that if I had entered that room from any place other than church, that scene would have ended very differently. Having God's Word freshly in my mind, heart, and spirit led me not to address a spiritual battle with a physical solution. My battle was not with my sister; it was against spiritual wickedness in high places influencing her.

Paul uses this text in Ephesians to remind us of the importance of being prepared for war. He uses the Roman soldier's armor to give a visual example of the tools that God has given us to fight this ongoing battle. Paul used a reference point that was relevant for his time. The emphasis is not on the armor, but what each protective component represents and its purpose. Paul begins by telling us to be strong in the Lord and in the power of His might. He is not expecting our strength to be generated by us or any other source; we are to stand in the power of God's might. Our might is no match for the battle we are fighting. Paul tells us to put on the whole armor of God because every piece has an important purpose.

*Our might is no match for the battle we are fighting.*

We are to put on the whole armor of God so that we can stand against the wiles or schemes of the Devil; without it, we are swaying, sitting, or knocked out. The Devil and his army are real; they are plotting for your demise. Some of the challenges you are facing are a direct result of the schemes he has created. When we think of schemes, we typically think of negative things that we can identify; but sometimes, they may appear in the form of a promotion that will decrease your time in the Word or church. Sometimes the scheme is a positive activity that will take up so much of your time that you neglect yourself, your health, and your family. Sometimes, the scheme is a handsome man with all the right words and a voice you can't wait to hear. Just know that God has given us what we need to stand.

We do not wrestle against flesh and blood (people). Yes, Satan uses people to carry out his schemes, but God wants you to know that the people are merely "the middlemen." The source is the Devil—spiritual wickedness in high places. This demonic army is organized and has a single focus on destroying what God created in His image, i.e., people.

You constantly hear of the destructive work of the Devil, and people often say, "The Devil is busy." "Yes, I agree, he is busy; he has declared war on God and God's people. God is totally aware of what is happening in your life and why. He has also given you tools to use that will enable you to stand. Equipping yourself with this armor will neither exempt you from battle scars nor wounds but guarantees your final status can read: STANDING.

*Equipping yourself with this armor will neither exempt you from battle scars nor wounds but guarantees your final status can read: STANDING.*

Now, let's examine our free wardrobe. The first piece of armor Paul tells us to put on is the belt of truth. He tells us to put on truth first because it serves several purposes. This belt covers the loins—an area of the body that is vital for survival. This belt also served as a place to hold the sword and the breastplate in place. Again, Paul was using these symbols because they were appropriate for his time, and people could connect the meaning.

Paul is emphasizing the importance of truth. If we are not honest with God and ourselves, the rest of the armor will be ineffective. When the truth is not your foundation, the picture we see of ourselves, others, and especially God is distorted. We put on truth by committing to learn and obey God's Word. *"If ye love me, keep my commandments"* (John 14:15 KJV). His Word is the truth; we must know it. Our priorities and decisions should begin with the truth of God's Word. Psalm 51:6 (KJV) states: *"Behold, thou desirest truth in my inward parts: in the hidden part thou shalt make me to know wisdom."*

Consider my rationale with Chester in the other chapter. In my mind, I had a valid reason for being disgusted by him. The truth of the matter was, I was harboring hatred in my heart. Furthermore, he had not committed an offense against me, and even if he had, God required me to forgive. David acknowledged the danger of harboring sin in our heart in Psalm 66:18, which says, *"If I regard iniquity in my heart, the Lord will not hear me."* We should live by this truth. God wants us to focus on the area that is not visible to the naked eye.

On a lighter note, I gave an example once when I taught this lesson about how I hate to see people texting and driving. Distracted driving is so dangerous! People who look away from the road to read a text for even a second can cause a tragic accident. At 55 mph, a person who looks away for 5 seconds can travel the length of a football field—blindfolded. The drivers look so careless and inconsiderate. But when I text and I drive, I am cautious to look up—often. The ladies all laughed at my illustration, but the truth was that I thought that we were not doing the same thing. It looked so bad when other people did it.

The truth of the matter is I was looking at the speck in their eyes but couldn't see the log in mine (Matthew 7:5). My actions were equally as dangerous as theirs; my driving was as distracted as theirs. Since then, my husband has placed a do-not-disturb app on my phone, and I no longer text and drive. God is longing to share the truth of His Word with you and provide you with the correct lens to view yourself, your situations, and His plan for your life.

*The truth of the matter is I was looking at the speck in their eyes but couldn't see the log in mine.*

The breastplate covered the heart; we know how vital this organ is to our survival. If an arrow or any other object pierces the heart, the person is in trouble. That injury can be fatal. The heart has several functions and is responsible for ensuring other parts of the body operate correctly. Paul tells us to put on the breastplate of righteousness. Romans 3:10 says, *"there is none righteous, no, not one."* This righteousness is the righteousness of Jesus, and we should thank God for the access He has granted to us. Jesus paid it all and because of His finished work on the cross, we are declared righteous before God.

Your goal as a Christian should be to know God's Word

and obey it. When you fall short, and you will, you can rely on the righteousness of Christ. The Devil, other people, and even you say things about yourself that are harmful. These negative words or descriptions can haunt you for years. Somehow, we manage to hold on to the negative words that are said about us but quickly forget the positive words. Spend time with God and face the truth about you; confess what you see and what God points out and walk in your forgiveness. You can stand when you know the breastplate you are wearing is the finished work of Jesus.

Paul talks about having your feet shod with the preparation of the gospel of peace. The emphasis is on the gospel. As Paul continues to refer to the wardrobe of Roman soldiers, you should know that they wore shoes that were spiked underneath. The spikes enabled them to be deeply planted, securing their footing. The soldiers had to walk in a precise way when wearing these cleated leather boots. The gospel should be our footing. What you believe is rooted in the gospel; it's your foundation. The life, the death, the burial, and the resurrection of Christ is what changed our destination from hell to Heaven. God wants us to be equipped in His Word and stable enough to confidently share it. The gospel gives peace, and we are commissioned to share its transforming power with the world. Whatever shoes you wear—whether heels, flats, or boots— look for opportunities to share the gospel of Jesus Christ and the peace it gives.

The shields used during this time, which were made of metal and wrapped in cowhide, were constructed in this manner to extinguish any darts on fire. Remember that the emphasis is on the function of the armor. During a battle, the enemy would use fiery darts as weapons, but the shield served not only to protect the soldier but also rendered the arrow ineffective. The arrow no longer presented a viable threat. Paul gives this illustration to demonstrate the protective power of faith.

When you know the truth of God's Word and decide to believe by faith that God is who He says He is and will always do what is in your best interest according to His plan, you can hold up your shield of faith and extinguish the fiery darts that are coming your way. Romans 10:17 (KJV) states, *"So then faith cometh by hearing, and hearing by the word of God."* Your faith is developed by hearing and listening to the Word of God. Since faith is strengthened through hearing the Word of God, listening to His Word should be a regular part of the Christians' lifestyle.

With all the technology to which we have access today, listening to God's Word is no longer challenging for most people. This means we should make listening to God's Word a regular practice. Reading the Word aloud also serves this purpose. The fiery darts will continue to come, but remember, *you control the quality of your shield by developing your faith.* Reading and listening to God's Word gives you examples of God's consistency and His character.

The helmet is used as a symbol to represent salvation. Paul uses the symbol of a helmet to convey the importance of this piece of armor as well. The helmet protects the brain, which controls our thoughts, memory, speech, movement of arms and legs, and many organs within the body. The reality of our salvation should serve as a helmet. The life Jesus lived on earth, His obedience to the Father, the torture He endured for our sakes, the power God used to raise Jesus from the dead, and the transformation that takes place once we accept Him as Savior is the helmet we should decide to guard our brain.

This knowledge should change your thoughts, help you go to God for the healing of your memories, influence your speech, dictate what your arms do and where your legs go. Salvation is a gift from God and is not meant to cease to have meaning in your life after you receive Jesus into your heart. This truth should serve as an ongoing part of your spiritual journey.

The sword of the Spirit, which is the Word of God is your offensive weapon. All the others serve as defensive weapons. The Word of God is the only weapon that will be effective against the schemes and fiery darts of the Devil. Since God's Word is what we fight with as Christians, consistent dosages are critical. Studying with tools and resources will provide the necessary references and background needed for a broader contextual understanding. Regular attendance in Bible study with faithful, God-fearing teachers will teach you how to apply the Word to your life. Also remember there is no substitute for the interpreting ability of the Holy Spirit. Before you read, ask God through His Spirit to lead you to the truth. God's Word was not written to frustrate you; God gave us His Word so that we could get to know Him. He longs to reveal Himself to us.

When you are stressing to come up with answers for your

life and feel like giving up, pull out your Sword and meditate on Proverbs 3:5 (KJV), which says, *"Trust in the LORD with all thine heart; and lean not unto thine own understanding."*

When you struggle with giving God a small portion of what He has given you, fight disobedience with Proverbs 3:9, which says, *"Honor the LORD with your wealth, with the firstfruits of all your crops."*

When tempted to betray someone's trust, use the Sword and remind yourself that Proverbs 11:13 says, *"A gossip betrays a confidence, but a trustworthy person keeps a secret."* Betrayal can become a way of life; take advantage of every opportunity to do the right thing. God has fixed it so we don't have to guess about what's right. It's all in His Word. Learn to use your Sword.

My friend, let's put on the whole armor. We need a specialized wardrobe to fight this battle. Let's get dressed!

*Father, we come acknowledging our helplessness before You. We confess that this life is hard to live without Your direction. Forgive us for continuing to live in our own strength. Thank You for providing us the tools to win the prayer battles that are before us. Remind us that we can't do anything significant without You, but with You, we can do all things through the strength You provide. In Jesus' name, I pray. Amen.*

# Operation Meditation

1. What comes to your mind about YOU when you read the passage, "God desires truth in our inward parts"?

2. What truth have you been denying? What truth do you need to confess to God?

3. How prepared are you to share the gospel? Is sharing this message a regular part of your lifestyle?

4. What are the areas that you need to allow the righteousness of Jesus to cover?

5. When under attack, what is the first spiritual weapon you employ?

# CHAPTER SEVEN

# Storms Can Build Stamina

S TORMS CAN BUILD stamina, or they can mask misery, breed bitterness, harden hearts, promote pity, or create a state of paralysis. As I was preparing to teach this lesson nearly fifteen years ago, I shared an illustration of what had happened to me during that week. I had taken both of my sons to the grocery store to buy a case of water. My youngest son, who was only eight but always looked for opportunities to show his physical strength, volunteered to carry the case of water to the car. I affectionately told him that while I appreciated his helpfulness, this was probably not a good idea. He insisted he could carry the water, and I knew that the only way to show him what I meant was to allow him to go as far as he could.

His older brother by two years would rather do anything other than something that required physical strength. In fact, he was standing back, hoping that I would not tell him to assist his brother. As my youngest son began to display a struggle with his task, his brother began to taunt him, saying, "You're not going to make it."

Of course, I verbally scolded my older son, but my youngest son replied (though he was nearly out of breath), "Go ahead, Mom. Let him talk. The more he talks, the stronger I get! It's okay; his talk is helping me."

As a mom, I had two issues. One issue was that I had a son who enjoyed seeing his younger brother struggle and did not go to his aid. The other issue was that my other son saw his older brother as his opposition. I had to wonder how long this dynamic had existed, what the best way was to address it, and what would happen if I treated the storms that I face with the attitude of my youngest son. He decidedly took the taunts of his brother as motivation to achieve a goal; he used negativism as a momentum for achieving something positive.

I used this situation as an illustration of the power of perspective. I knew God wanted to remind me and tell others that the outcome or the prevailing attitude of a storm is totally dependent on the person experiencing the storm. I experienced some storms the same way I endured roller coasters—with my eyes closed and only coming along for the ride. Yes, I was on the ride, but I didn't see anything; consequently, my experience was limited. In this same way, I have gone through some storms with my eyes shut and holding my breath, waiting for it to pass. I must confess, I didn't learn anything about myself or God during those times. But guess what? These same storms with different names continued to come my way, and I kept asking God, "Why do I keep going through all of these things?"

*I have gone through some storms with my eyes shut and holding my breath, waiting for it to pass.*

One week was like a dust storm, another week was a thunderstorm, the next week was a windstorm, the next week an ice storm. I began to understand that while the elements of those storms were different, my lesson was the same. My realization was like hearing God say, "If you don't pass the tests, you repeat the course." There is no *social promotion* (an educational term employed when students are promoted to the next grade without mastering the skills needed in the previous grade) with God.

I was looking for peace in my storms. Well, I called what I wanted peace, but in truth, I was looking for the absence of any conflict. However, Jesus told us in John 16:33, *"I have told you these things, so that in me you may have peace. In this world, you will have trouble. But take heart! I have overcome the world."* The New Living Translation puts it this way: *"I have told you all this so that you may have peace in me. Here on earth you will have many trials and sorrows. But take heart because I have overcome the world."* In other words, this notion of having a problem-free life should not exist, right?

Intellectually, I knew the truth of this verse, but I kept waiting for this life anyway—until I experienced a storm that almost cost me the life of my child. I had allowed the stress of infidelity in a marriage to consume me to the point that I had several threats of miscarriage. Eventually, to save my child's life, my doctor ordered me on bedrest. This storm was the one that taught me how to surrender and seek the Savior. I used this bedrest time to study (not just *read*) God's Word. I needed God's help, and I knew it. Additionally, I wrote lessons God was teaching me about Himself, human nature, sin, prayer, faith, forgiveness, and obedience. My period of bedrest lasted for five months, but the benefits filled six journals with messages from God and a healthy son weighing nine pounds and one ounce.

### Matthew 14:22-33

*Immediately Jesus made the disciples get into the boat and go on ahead of him to the other side, while he dismissed the crowd. ²³After he had dismissed them, he went up on the mountainside by himself to pray. Later that night, he was there alone, ²⁴and the boat was already a considerable distance from land, buffeted by the waves because the wind was against it.*

*²⁵**Shortly before dawn**, Jesus went out to them, walking on the lake.*

*²⁶When the disciples saw him walking on the lake, were terrified. "It's a ghost," they said, cried out in fear.*

*²⁷But Jesus immediately said to them: "Take courage! It is I. Don't be afraid."*

*²⁸"Lord, if it's you," Peter replied, "tell me to come to you on the water."*

*²⁹"Come," he said. Then Peter got down out of the boat, walked on the water and came toward Jesus. ³⁰But when he saw the wind, he was afraid and, beginning to sink, cried out, "Lord, save me!"*

*³¹Immediately Jesus reached out his hand and caught him. "You of little faith," he said, "why did you doubt?"*

*³²And when they climbed into the boat, the wind died down. ³³Then those who were in the boat worshiped him, saying, "Truly you are the Son of God."*

While this Scripture passage may be very familiar to some, God's Word is full of light. Allow God to speak to you heart and your mind. In this passage, Jesus sent the disciples in the direction of a storm, but He gave them a destination point. The goal was to get to the other side of the water. Likewise, it is important for you to remember what God said He would do for, in, or through you when storms commence. Jesus did not immediately go to the disciples. The Bible tells us that He took time to go pray. Spending time with God, the Father, was a priority for God, the Son.

*The quality of your life is affected by your commitment to spending time with God, i.e., speaking and listening to Him.*

Friend, if you don't remember anything else from this book, remember that the quality of your life is affected by your commitment to spending time with God, i.e., speaking and listening to Him. The disciples were people, exactly like you and me. The Bible tells us that the boat was far from the land, and they were experiencing turbulence in the boat. In other words, they are in a predicament.

I wonder what they were thinking or if they even started sharing suppositions with each other:

- "He knew this storm was coming; that's why He's not in the boat."

- "He tricked us into setting sail for the other side."

- "He lied to us; He said He was going to join us. There's no way He can join us now."

- "What was so important back there that He forgot about us?"
- "I should have known following Him was gonna get us killed one day."

Sometimes, we need to be destination-driven. The destination is not always physical; sometimes the destination is emotional, mental, and always spiritual. We must understand that He who has begun a good work in us is faithful to complete it (Philippians 1:6).

Can you relate to the disciples' situation? Have you ever been in a situation that looked hopeless? The Bible says, *"Shortly before dawn..."* (v. 25). What? He waited several hours to join them? That verse adds, *"Jesus went out to them, **walking** on the lake."* What? Walking? The disciples are going through a storm; they are far from land, and Jesus is *walking*—not jogging nor running, but *walking*. Clearly, the disciples were not singing and praying at the time. They were afraid and cried out that what they saw was a ghost.

However, I cannot make that assumption because I am guilty of singing and praying, and minutes later, I looked at something that brought me fear. I've been in church worshipping when a thought about some care of my life only to be overtaken with anxiety, stress, and worry. I left worship mentally and began trying to make my own way out of situations.

I probably looked like I was taking notes from the sermon, but I was trying to make plans "B," "C," and "D." I thank God for all the times He responded to me with the same words He gave the disciples: "Take courage. Don't be afraid, it's Me." The Bible says, "IMMEDIATELY," He spoke to them (v. 27). Something is wonderfully calming about His voice, and His timing is perfect.

Apparently, Peter desired more than peace in the boat. He asked Jesus for an opportunity to experience more. Some translations use the word empower or command instead of "tell me." Peter was specific in his request. He told Jesus that he wanted to walk on the water too. He believed that, according to his request, Jesus could make this happen.

As I studied this passage, I wondered what the conversation must have been like among those watching from the boat. What did the disciples say to themselves? What did they say to each other? What did they say as Peter was stepping out of the boat?

Did they say the following?

- "Peter, it sounds like Jesus. Sit down and wait for Him."

- "Go on out there; we'll be praying for you!"

- "He did say come, but I'm not yet at that level of faith."

Peter didn't say, "Empower us to come to You on the water." He kept his request personal. There are times when you will need to be like the friends who peeled back the roof to lower their friend down to Jesus for healing (Luke 5:17-39). Many others who knew when Jesus was in town also took their sick and diseased to him (Luke 4:40). There are also times, as we see with Peter, that your focus must be on your relationship with Jesus—even if it means leaving some others behind.

Jesus spoke one word to Peter, and His simple directive was, *"Come."* Jesus didn't make a persuasive speech for Peter, Jesus didn't give him a pep talk, Jesus didn't even warn Peter that the trek to Him would be harder than it looked. He just said, *"Come."*

Jesus didn't call anyone's name. Does this mean all of them could have stepped into the stormy waters and experienced this same miracle? Was He only talking to Peter? Were any of the others tempted to get up and take Jesus at His word? Did Peter look at the other disciples and say, "Guys, He said, 'Come.' Let's go."

Did the disciples respond by saying, "No way, big mouth, you were the one who wanted to join Him. You go right ahead; He's talking to you"?

I don't know the answer to these questions, but I do know that Peter responded to His Lord's invitation. His action was based on Jesus' solitary word: *"Come."* The voice of Jesus and the one word spoken gave him the power to do the unthinkable. This account defies gravity. I have heard this passage preached several times and have heard people say that Peter took his eyes off Jesus, but the Bible doesn't say that Peter ever saw Jesus. The Bible tells us that (at some point) Peter saw the wind and became fearful.

I was a very judgmental new Christian and still relapse occasionally. When I originally read this passage, I thought, *How could he have been afraid when Jesus was right there? He's walking on water after all!*

Then it was as if I heard God clear His throat again. Jesus

lives inside of me in the person of the Holy Spirit, and I still get scared. I've had my own figuratively walking-on-water experiences and still battle fear. My view of Peter changed immediately. I saw videoclips in my brain of my fearing, and as a result, sinking. I wanted to delete that slideshow, but I really needed to view it. Simply because Jesus empowers you or commands you to do something or leads you in a particular direction doesn't mean it will be "wind-free." Understanding that winds will blow but your deliverance will come in continuously hearing God's voice is important.

## The Rescue

Peter's response to the wind was wrong, but his response to sinking was right. He recognized who Jesus was, he called him "Lord," and he made his request known: "Save me." Peter didn't hold his breath and prepare for the worse. When you make a mistake, doubt or fear, don't become a martyr. Do not say to yourself, "I deserve whatever comes to me." Call on the Lord and tell Him you need Him again. Peter was a fisherman, which means he probably knew how to swim, yet he looked to Jesus for help. God doesn't want you to make your own way; it's His desire to deliver. I find myself adding another word to Peter's prayer: "Lord, save me again." Take note: God's deliverance will, more than likely, look very different from the vision you may create.

The Bible gives us Jesus' timing: *immediately* Jesus reached out His hand. Peter initiated the rescue by calling out and asking to be saved, but Jesus was the One who performed the rescue.

## The Rebuke

However, this story doesn't end with the rescue; a rebuke follows. There is value in open rebuke. Psalm 27:5 (KJV) states, *"Open rebuke is better than secret love."* Jesus told Peter his faith was little.

I don't know what Peter was thinking, but I wonder if it was anything like, "Little? What do you mean, little faith? At least I got out of the boat! The **little** faith fishermen are still in the boat. I can't wait to hear how you are going to reprimand them when we get back. If my faith is little, then they better get fired. Little, Lord? Really? Do I get any credit for the one-way trip I made on the water? Do You remember anything before I saw the wind and began to sink? Seems to me like You would address my strengths before You start to talk about my weakness. I can't wait to get back to this boat and hear what You are going to say the *boat keepers.* Can we run back?"

Of course, this self-dialogue is all my imagination because I put myself in Peter's shoes, and that's the scenario I imagined. If you spend your time looking for affirmation for an incomplete assignment, you run the risk of never experiencing the magnitude of the miracle. When God gives you a command, anything short of completing it may earn you the "little faith talk."

For the record, the rebuke didn't end there. Jesus followed this statement with a question. I'm proud of Peter for not trying to answer this unanswerable question. Maybe he thought, *Jesus is standing on water; His word empowered me to walk on water. It's probably safe to say that if He can defy gravity, He*

___

*knows I doubted without my verbalizing it.* Jesus asked Peter why he doubted.

God's questions are always rhetorical. Remember God's conversation with Adam in Genesis 3:9? Adam and Eve had sinned, and Adam attempted to hide from God, although this is impossible. God asked Adam, "Where are you?" Of course, God knew Adam's exact location; again, this question is rhetorical. God wanted Adam to see what Adam was doing. *"Who told you were naked? Have you eaten of the tree of which I commanded you not to eat?"* (v. 11). Then the Lord asked Eve a question: *"What is this that you have done?"* (v. 13). God's questions are designed to disarm, deprogram, develop, and ultimately deliver us.

Notice that God did not ask the serpent any questions. Why do you think God didn't question the serpent? Another example of God's questioning as a tool for reflection to lead to repentance in His conversation with Job?

### Job 38:4-41 (NASB)

*"Where were you when I laid the foundation of the earth? Tell Me, if you have understanding, ⁵Who set its measurements? Since you know. Or who stretched the line on it? ⁶"On what were its bases sunk? Or who laid its cornerstone, ⁷When the morning stars sang together and all the sons of God shouted for joy?*

*⁸"Or who enclosed the sea with doors When, bursting forth, it went out from the womb; ⁹When I made a cloud its garment And thick darkness its swaddling band,*

___

¹⁰*And I placed boundaries on it And set a bolt and doors,* ¹¹*And I said, 'Thus far you shall come, but no farther; And here shall your proud waves stop'?*

¹²*"Have you ever in your life commanded the morning, And caused the dawn to know its place,* ¹³*That it might take hold of the ends of the earth, And the wicked be shaken out of it?* ¹⁴*"It is changed like clay under the seal; And they stand forth like a garment.* ¹⁵*"From the wicked their light is withheld, And the uplifted arm is broken.*

¹⁶*"Have you entered into the springs of the sea Or walked in the recesses of the deep?* ¹⁷*"Have the gates of death been revealed to you, Or have you seen the gates of deep darkness?* ¹⁸*"Have you understood the expanse of the earth? Tell Me, if you know all this.*

¹⁹*"Where is the way to the dwelling of light? And darkness, where is its place,* ²⁰*That you may take it to its territory And that you may discern the paths to its home?* ²¹*"You know, for you were born then, And the number of your days is great!* ²²*"Have you entered the storehouses of the snow, Or have you seen the storehouses of the hail,* ²³*Which I have reserved for the time of distress, For the day of war and battle?* ²⁴*"Where is the way that the light is divided, Or the east wind scattered on the earth?*

²⁵*"Who has cleft a channel for the flood, Or a way for the thunderbolt,* ²⁶*To bring rain on a land without people, On a desert without a man in it,* ²⁷*To satisfy the waste and desolate land And to make the seeds of grass*

to sprout? ²⁸"Has the rain a father? Or who has begotten the drops of dew? ²⁹"From whose womb has come the ice? And the frost of heaven, who has given it birth? ³⁰"Water becomes hard like stone, And the surface of the deep is imprisoned.

³¹"Can you bind the chains of the Pleiades, Or loose the cords of Orion? ³²"Can you lead forth a constellation in its season, And guide the Bear with her satellites? ³³"Do you know the ordinances of the heavens, Or fix their rule over the earth?

³⁴"Can you lift up your voice to the clouds, So that an abundance of water will cover you? ³⁵"Can you send forth lightnings that they may go And say to you, 'Here we are'? ³⁶"Who has put wisdom in the innermost being Or given understanding to the mind? ³⁷"Who can count the clouds by wisdom, Or tip the water jars of the heavens, ³⁸When the dust hardens into a mass And the clods stick together?

³⁹"Can you hunt the prey for the lion, Or satisfy the appetite of the young lions, ⁴⁰When they crouch in their dens And lie in wait in their lair? ⁴¹"Who prepares for the raven its nourishment When its young cry to God And wander about without food?

Have you heard God ask you any questions lately? When He does, friend, take the time to ponder and then answer them. Doing so is to your advantage; remember God knows everything, and the answer will benefit you.

*While rebuke may follow your rescue, don't continue to hide from God or resist calling on Him to save you.*

While rebuke may follow your rescue, don't continue to hide from God or resist calling on Him to save you. Psalm 121:1, *"I will lift up mine eyes unto the hills, from whence cometh my help. My help cometh from the LORD, which made heaven and earth."*

The Bible doesn't shed light on how Jesus and Peter got back to the boat, but the passage does say in verse 32: *"they both climbed into the boat...."* The Bible doesn't say, "Jesus climbed into the boat and sat Peter down," so I think it's safe to say that Jesus didn't climb into the boat carrying Peter in His arms or on His back.

## The Repositioning

God gave Peter the opportunity to get back on top of that in which he was once sinking. Peter resumed his initial position of walking on the water while the wind continued to blow. How do I know? The Bible said, *"And when they climbed into the boat, the wind died down"* (v. 32). The physical element that caused Peter to fear was the wind; Jesus did not remove the element. Peter developed the faith to walk on the water despite the wind. You may be waiting for God to cause the wind to cease before you walk, but God may be waiting on you to walk before He causes the wind to cease.

According to verse 33, when Peter and Jesus returned to the boat, the disciples worshipped Jesus, confessing that He was truly the Son of God. I confessed earlier that I was judgmental, and yes, I was angry at the disciples for having amnesia. After all, He had just fed 5,000 men (not to mention the women and children) with only two fish and five loaves of bread! Apparently, this miracle didn't prove to them that He was truly the Son of God.

It wasn't long before I heard (not audibly) God clear His throat yet again. He reminded me that the Bible exposes the weaknesses of believers to help me see myself and my tendencies. He wants me to remember that nothing good exists in my flesh (Romans 7:18). I have also experienced miracles from God but was plagued by drastic memory loss at the next challenge. In an effort to walk away from the light of God's Word with a better understanding of Him and ourselves, let's plan to keep pen and paper or electronic device in hand when we study God's Word. We should start taking some "spiritual selfies."

*Lord, thank You for this time together. I pray that You will make this passage and the lessons learned from this passage a very real part of my sister-in-Christ's life. Help her to trust that You love her and that in everything You allow her to experience, You will be right there. Remind her that You know the end of her story and have given her everything she needs to run this race, and it's in Your Word. Lord, help her to call on You when she is afraid, if she starts to sink, allow her to feel Your touch during the rescue. In the name of Jesus, I pray. Amen.*

# Operation Meditation

1. As you think about the passage studied in Matthew 14:22-33, list an example when you identified with Peter and one when you identified with the disciples who remained in the boat.

2. What is your "wind"—that which you are watching that may be causing things to shift and move in your life?

3. What is your water—that on which you once walked but now feel pulling you under?

4. Jesus made prayer a priority; how do you plan to institute this discipline in your life?

5. When you feel like Jesus is "walking" instead of "running" to your side, what will you remind yourself?

6. According to this text, was Jesus angry with His disciples for being afraid?

7. Are you comfortable telling God you are afraid?

8. What is your first response when you are afraid?

9. Fill in this blank. When I hear the voice of _____, it evokes emotions that I can't control. When I hear the concern in their voice, I usually cry.

10. Fill in this blank. Because I trust _____ so much, I would practically do anything for him/her.

11. Jesus told Peter to "Come." What is He saying to you?

12. From what do you need Jesus to rescue you?

13. Describe your last storm. How would you describe your response?

# CHAPTER EIGHT

# You're Too Late

W HEN MY SONS were growing up, they were fairly simple kids in their wants and desires for material things. They did not ask for much though I did refuse to purchase a few things because of the price. The point came in their lives when they wanted things and vowed to pay me later if I purchased them. I didn't need long to see that once they received their desired purchase, the motivation to pay disappeared.

One of them wanted some very expensive tennis shoes. I determined that he needed to earn and save his own money to purchase them because, in my opinion, they were too pricey. When the shoes went on sale, my son reminded me for an entire week of the "one-day-only" sale for these shoes he desired. Not only was this a one-day sale, the hours for the sale were limited. I agreed that I would try to leave work in time to get to the mall within the time frame.

When I awakened the morning of the sale, I found a post-it note on the mirror of bathroom, one on my bedroom door, one on the garage door that I would see on my way to my car, another one in the car, and the last one was in my work briefcase. Every post-it note had the same message: "Mom, the sale ends at 4:00; leave work by 3." I also received a couple of phone calls while at work with this same message.

My son's persistence was impressive; he had saved his own money, and I was looking forward to observing him receive the fruit of his labor. I left work and arrived home at 5:30; several unexpected meetings had lasted beyond my planned time to leave work. I expected him to be waiting outside for me, but he was not. Then I thought as soon as he heard the garage door open, he would run to the car ready to go to the store, but he did not. Then I thought when I entered the house, he would run to me ready to go, but he did not.

I finally found him in his room, despondent, upset, and disappointed. He reminded me of all the things he did right:

- "I earned the money, and I saved it."
- "I watched for the sale."
- "I left several notes to remind you everywhere, and I even called you at work."

To top it all off, he added, "Mom, I would never do that to you." I could see the pain etched in his face, but he was straddling the fence of disrespect. My presence meant nothing to him.

I remember asking him the name of the store again, and he looked at me long enough not to say what he was really thinking. Instead, his agitated response was "It doesn't matter what the name of the store is now. The sale is over. You came home too late. Mom, if you really cared, you would have followed the directions on my notes."

Fifteen years later, this incident and the resulting confrontation is still sketched in my brain for several reasons.

1) I won't forget the pain etched in his face.

2) I know how close he came to getting something other than the tennis shoes.

3) I was insulted that it never crossed his mind that my resources were greater than his resources.

The shoes needed to be on sale for him to purchase them, but I was not limited by the original price of the shoe. He had relegated me to the same category that he was in! I had a job, I drove a car, I had credit cards, I had a checking and savings account; he had none of those. I was his sole provider, yet he did not remember any of my past provisions. He was solely focused on the end time of the sale. All his hopes had died at 4:00. My presence didn't resurrect any hope. "You're too late" continued to ring in my head.

To make a long story short, I said, "Get in the car." He sulkily obeyed, and we drove to the mall to buy the shoes. My plan was to prove to my son that I was not bound by the same limitations that he had and that my resources could handle the retail price. I wanted him to know that while many things will be impossible for him, they will not be impossible for me.

*My plan was to prove to my son that I was not bound by the same limitations that he had.*

### John 11:1-40 (KJV)

*Now a certain man was sick, named Lazarus, of Bethany, the town of Mary and her sister Martha. ²(It was that Mary which anointed the Lord with ointment, and wiped his feet with her hair, whose brother Lazarus was sick.)*

³*Therefore his sisters sent unto him, saying, Lord, behold, he whom thou lovest is sick.*

⁴*When Jesus heard that, he said, This sickness is not unto death, but for the glory of God, that the Son of God might be glorified thereby. ⁵Now Jesus loved Martha, and her sister, and Lazarus. ⁶When he had heard therefore that he was sick, he abode two days still in the same place where he was. ⁷Then after that saith he to his disciples, Let us go into Judaea again.*

⁸*His disciples say unto him, Master, the Jews of late sought to stone thee; and goest thou thither again?*

⁹*Jesus answered, Are there not twelve hours in the day? If any man walk in the day, he stumbleth not, because he seeth the light of this world. ¹⁰But if a man walk in the night, he stumbleth, because there is no light in him. ¹¹These things said he: and after that he saith unto them, Our friend Lazarus sleepeth; but I go, that I may awake him out of sleep.*

¹²*Then said his disciples, Lord, if he sleep, he shall do well.*

¹³*Howbeit Jesus spake of his death: but they thought that he had spoken of taking of rest in sleep. ¹⁴Then said Jesus unto them plainly, Lazarus is dead. ¹⁵And I am glad for your sakes that I was not there, to the intent ye may believe; nevertheless let us go unto him.*

¹⁶*Then said Thomas, which is called Didymus, unto his fellow disciples, Let us also go, that we may die with him.*

¹⁷*Then when Jesus came, he found that he had lain*

in the grave four days already. [18]Now Bethany was nigh unto Jerusalem, about fifteen furlongs off: [19]And many of the Jews came to Martha and Mary, to comfort them concerning their brother. [20]Then Martha, as soon as she heard that Jesus was coming, went and met him: but Mary sat still in the house. [21]Then said Martha unto Jesus, Lord, if thou hadst been here, my brother had not died. [22]But I know, that even now, whatsoever thou wilt ask of God, God will give it thee.

[23]Jesus saith unto her, Thy brother shall rise again.

[24]Martha saith unto him, I know that he shall rise again in the resurrection at the last day.

[25]Jesus said unto her, I am the resurrection, and the life: he that believeth in me, though he were dead, yet shall he live: [26]And whosoever liveth and believeth in me shall never die. Believest thou this?

[27]She saith unto him, Yea, Lord: I believe that thou art the Christ, the Son of God, which should come into the world. [28]And when she had so said, she went her way, and called Mary her sister secretly, saying, The Master is come, and calleth for thee. [29]As soon as she heard that, she arose quickly, and came unto him.

[30]Now Jesus was not yet come into the town, but was in that place where Martha met him. [31]The Jews then which were with her in the house, and comforted her, when they saw Mary, that she rose up hastily and went out, followed her, saying, She goeth unto the grave to weep there. [32]Then when Mary was come where Jesus

*was, and saw him, she fell down at his feet, saying unto him, Lord, if thou hadst been here, my brother had not died.*

*[33] When Jesus therefore saw her weeping, and the Jews also weeping which came with her, he groaned in the spirit, and was troubled. [34] And said, Where have ye laid him? They said unto him, Lord, come and see. [35] Jesus wept.*

*[36] Then said the Jews, Behold how he loved him! [37] And some of them said, Could not this man, which opened the eyes of the blind, have caused that even this man should not have died?*

*[38] Jesus therefore again groaning in himself cometh to the grave. It was a cave, and a stone lay upon it.* [This picture will be seen again.] *[39] Jesus said, Take ye away the stone. Martha, the sister of him that was dead, saith unto him, Lord, by this time he stinketh: for he hath been dead four days. [40] Jesus saith unto her, Said I not unto thee, that, if thou wouldest believe, thou shouldest see the glory of God?*

This passage begins by sharing the background of Mary and Martha, two sisters who lived with their brother in Bethany. God highlights Mary's history with Jesus; she had anointed His feet and then wiped them with her hair. The text seems to suggest that the sisters had an expectation of Jesus. They sent him a note informing Jesus that Lazarus was sick and reminded Jesus of His feelings for their brother—as if Jesus needed to be reminded of His relationship with Lazarus.

In our day, this reminder is like my son's calling me and saying, "Mom, your granddaughter wants to do gymnastics." He has placed an emphasis on my relationship with her, which, in his mind, guarantees that his request will be granted (and it will). But because our ways are not His and His ways are not ours, this ploy didn't work on Jesus (Isaiah 55:8, 9). He did not change His agenda to run to their sides.

God knows our frames, and I'm glad He inserted the line that reaffirms that Jesus loved all three—not just Lazarus. The disciples are puzzled by Jesus' response; they remind Him that Bethany is the place where He was almost stoned and questioned His return to the scene of the "almost crime." Jesus gives them the game plan: "Lazarus is sleeping. Let's go change his condition." The disciples don't get the same game plan, and their response proves it. They basically say, "Of course he will wake up if he's asleep."

In my mind's eye, I can see Jesus scratching His head and taking a deep breath before saying to them, "Okay, listen; he's not sleeping. He's *dead*, guys. And your response lets me know that Mary and Martha aren't the only ones who need to see this to believe" (my paraphrase, of course).

Then Thomas said to other disciples, "Let's join Jesus on this trip. They didn't kill Him the first time but will certainly succeed this time. But, hey, we are a team; let's go die with Him" (emphasis mine).

Martha met Jesus with that famous line, *"if you had been here, my brother would not have died"* (v. 21). She didn't understand to whom she was talking, and when Jesus tried to remind her, she wasn't listening. She basically responded (in today's vernacular), "Yeah, yeah, I know. I'll see him again when we are all dead."

When Mary sees Jesus, she then questions her Savior with almost the same words as her sister. This response may be result of the conversation that has taken place over the last four days. She also believes that Jesus is too late—*like my son believed.* The sight of Mary and the other hopeless mourners deeply grieved Jesus.

His response (in my mind) was, "Where is Lazarus? Y'all still need to see miracles, and I need to prove Myself yet again."

The grievers walk Jesus to the burial ground as proof He was too late. There Jesus wept. The Jews interpreted His crying as evidence of His love for Lazarus. They were wrong.

How do you handle consistently being misunderstood? When we underestimate WHO God is and believe that He is ever too late, all the conclusions we draw will be incorrect.

Some of those who were dealing with their grief then turned their criticism into a question. "How is it that He can make the blind see, but He cannot keep Lazarus from dying? That's weird, huh?" (v. 37).

Jesus was deeply moved again and then gives the command, "Remove the stone" (v. 39).

Martha, still focused on what she thinks was the deadline (four days ago), seeks to inform Jesus of the condition of Lazarus' body. Though she called Jesus, *"Lord,"* which means "Jehovah," she still thought she knew something that He didn't. In other words, she was saying, "Lord, You're too late. You should have come while he was sick! There's nothing You can do now—His body stinks."

I wasn't there, but I have never heard anyone say the words, "Didn't I tell you?" in a *soft* voice. But this is Jesus, and His tone doesn't really matter though He does remind Martha of His preciously spoken word, and that's what we should all remember.

*Lord, thank You for Your Word that has the power to heal, direct, re-direct, de-program, re-program, convict, and encourage us all. Help my friend to remember that You not only know everything, see everything, and control everything, but you also love her. God, we are so used to walking by sight and basing our emotions and decisions on things that we understand that we oftentimes limit You. Please forgive her. Increase her time of listening to Your Word, which is the tool you have given her to develop her faith. The next time she is tempted to give up, please use the power of Your Word to remind her that it is impossible for You to be late. In Jesus' name, I pray. Amen.*

# Operation Meditation

1. Can you see the correlation between my son's response and the response of Mary and Martha?

2. Can you see yourself?

3. Do you have a pain that you think is too late for God to address?

4. As you read this chapter, did you identify a time when you defined God by your limited vision and resources?

5. Complete this sentence: Jesus, if You had been here, _____would not have happened.

6. Ask God to show you some conclusions you may have drawn in error. Journal them and discuss them with a trusted, mature (in the Word, not age) Christian mentor.

# CHAPTER NINE

# Lord, I Lost *Me*

W HEN I WAS growing up, I thought deeply about my identity; I often wondered about the purpose of my existence. I tried to focus on my strengths in order to create a foundation for my self-worth. However, it didn't take long before I found somebody else with the same attribute. People in my neighborhood often complimented me on the length of my hair and the color of my eyes. Well, by the time I entered high school, I noticed hundreds of girls fit that same description. As a matter of fact, several even had longer hair and eyes that were equally as pretty.

Rather subtly, the comparison game had begun in my life. I had thick hair but wanted thin hair because, in my opinion, it was bouncier and easier to manage. I measured a 36C cup in the ninth grade, but I wanted much smaller ones. I thought girls with smaller busts looked better in their clothes. I was outgoing but secretly wanted to be the quiet girl; in my estimation, teachers seemed to like the quiet ones more. By high school, I was five feet, two inches in height, which never changed; I wanted to be taller. This comparison list could go on and on, but I'll stop here.

The point is, finding the real me was a long, painful journey. I can even remember the place where I lost what was left

*Finding the real me was a long, painful journey.* of me. I was 23 years old, married, pregnant, and we had moved to a state where I knew no one. While, I would have liked to change several things about my family (and I'm sure the feeling was mutual), at times I missed the familiarity. I felt as if life was demanding that I become something and somebody else to fit in the new experience called marriage and ministry.

Finally, the day came when I had to ask myself a series of questions. I was embarrassed, but knew I needed to get through this process of not simply asking myself questions but dealing with the answers that were to come.

- Who am I really?
- What do I like?
- How do I like my hair?
- What is my personal dress style?
- What am I doing because others expect me to do it?
- How do I really feel about my current situation?
- How has my past influenced my present?
- In what ways am I like some of the people in my family who I criticize?
- Others have chosen drugs to anesthetize their pain, what is my anesthesia?
- How much of my life am I living for others?
- Whose opinions am I valuing?

- How much of my image is accurate? In other words, how much of what people say about me, is true?

- Do I love people, or do I tolerate them?

- Did Jesus love people or tolerate them?

- How valuable is my time with God, really?

- If God gave my eulogy, what would he have to say?

- Who is God calling me to be?

- Is my normal, *normal*?

This partial list contains only a few of the therapeutic questions about me I decided to address. I believe in the power of reflecting with God for He has healed me from the inside, out.

**2 Kings 6:1-7 (KJV)**

*And the sons of the prophets said unto Elisha, Behold now, the place where we dwell with thee is too strait for us. ²Let us go, we pray thee, unto Jordan, and take thence every man a beam, and let us make us a place there, where we may dwell. And he answered, Go ye.*

*³And one said, Be content, I pray thee, and go with thy servants. And he answered, I will go. ⁴So he went with them. And when they came to Jordan, they cut down wood.*

*⁵But as one was felling a beam, the axe head fell into the water: and he cried, and said, Alas, master! for it was borrowed.*

*⁶And the man of God said, Where fell it? And he*

*shewed him the place. And he cut down a stick, and cast it in thither; and the iron did swim.*

*⁷Therefore said he, Take it up to thee. And he put out his hand, and took it.*

This lesson from the life of Elisha focuses on a college training for prophets. The one spoken of in the passage seems to be at Gilgal. Because of the work God was doing through Elisha, many of the sons of prophets wanted to be near him. Their numbers increased, and the space where they lived had become too small for them. The prophets went to Elisha, their leader, and voiced the need to expand their facilities. They told Elisha that they were willing to go and cut trees themselves to build more homes, but they insisted that he be present.

This need for their leader reminds me of the refrain of the old hymn that says, "If Jesus goes with me, I'll go anywhere." This account is another example (the first being the woman who had given up hope) of God's using Elisha to demonstrate the compassion God has for His children. Elisha's presence was again required because of the sensitivity he possessed for God's people. God desires for His children to trust Him in such a way that they will desire and believe that His presence is always enough; His presence alone should give security.

While this passage in the Bible is very short, the lessons that can be gleaned from it can be life-changing. Unfortunately, we tend to take too many things for granted. Remembering that while God is everywhere all the time, it is also critically imperative that we are cognizant of our need for Him even in what may seem to be casual, everyday activities. Consciously acknowledge His presence and invite Him everywhere you go—*not* because He needs your permission to go—but because you recognize the importance of his presence.

I used to hear people pray for "traveling grace." In my experiences, this prayer was a recognition and admittance of needing God for safe travel; however, I don't hear that prayer prayed much anymore. Maybe it's because we rely on our nice, high-tech cars or our cell phones that are all equipped with a global positioning system (GPS). Let's return to relying on God for our very existence. I am not writing this as one who has mastered this goal—quite the contrary.

*Remembering that while God is everywhere all the time, it is also critically imperative that we are cognizant of our need for Him even in what may seem to be casual, everyday activities.*

Not too long ago, I was driving with my mom, who can't drive and will never get out and pump gas (but notorious for demanding the driver maintain at least a half tank). She continually watched the gas gauge and annoyingly repeated the need for me to stop for gas. I did not stop because my mother is not as tech-savvy as I am and was underestimating my "smart" car that warns me when I am getting low on gas and will even direct me to the nearest gas station if I so desire. Well, my *smart* car did not tell me that the next gas station was farther than the amount of gas remaining in the tank. Suddenly, my mom was looking like the smartest person in the car.

My mom could tell by the look on my face that something

was wrong—because I did not have the courage to admit that I should have listened to her. I began to pray because not only did I not see a gas station in sight, I didn't see anything other than land and trees. Trust me, I was really praying without ceasing. Then it dawned on me that although I needed gas, my need for God did not increase; I needed Him just as much as when the gas tank read full. Sadly, I didn't recognize that need.

The prophet-in-training recognized and voiced a need for Elisha's presence. No matter what position you may hold in life or even in the church, there is never a time when you do not need God. Even in the tasks you may consider routine, menial, and insignificant, be sure you have Him with you.

The prophet was chopping down a tree, doing a good deed, and helping to better the prophet community when the tool broke and the axe head fell into the water. Note, the first thing the prophet-in-training did was cry out to Elisha, who represents God in this illustration. The man did not blame the axe. He didn't blame the owner of the axe for giving him a faulty tool.

*Sometimes, discussions delay or terminate deliverance.* When something breaks in your life, are you quick to look for external factors to blame? Do you feel a need to declare to the world or anyone who will listen that it wasn't your fault? Do you feel like you need to justify the loss to God? Not this man! He cried out to Elisha and expressed his main concern: the axe had been borrowed. He was concerned about what happened to something that was in his possession that did not belong to him. Oh, the friendships that might still be intact today if people would have treated the things loaned to them with the type of care this man showed, but I digress.

The man immediately took his problem to Elisha. The axe head was iron, so he was probably not counting on getting it back. After all, everyone knows that if metal falls into water, the bottom of the water is its destiny. Nevertheless, his instinct was to call on the prophet. The passage above stated that Elisha asked the man to show him where he lost the axe head.

Notice that Elisha did not ask the humiliating, rhetorical questions that most people dread hearing:

"How in the world did you ever lose an axe head?"

"What were you thinking about while you were swinging that axe?"

"Don't you know you could have hurt yourself and others?"

No, Elisha did not care about how the prophet-in-training lost it.

Whatever you are facing in your life that may seem like a lost cause or an impossibility, take it to God and trust Him. God placed this unnamed man in the Bible to demonstrate to us how much He loves and cares for us and about the matters that concern us. Acts 10:34, *"Then Peter began to speak: 'I now realize how true it is that God does not show favoritism.'"* Taking our problems that appear to be permanently lost requires faith. Hebrews 11:6 (KJV), *"But without faith it is impossible to please him: for he that cometh to God must believe that he is, and that he is a rewarder of them that diligently seek him."* This is the time to denounce pride and self-pity, to confess lack, and to admit the loss. God will address every need in your life that you take to Him.

When Elisha directed the prophet to take him to the place, he obeyed. When God gives you a directive, immediate obedience is required for best results. Elisha cut part of a limb and tossed it into the water, and the axe head floated to the top. What? Iron floated?! Yes, God suspended the natural order of gravity to assist this man. Then Elisha told the man to lift the axe head out of the water and continue working. God always has a part for us to play. He could have made the axe head return to dry ground. He could have made the axe head appear in the man's hand. But God isn't into magic; He allows us to be participants in the miracle. For example, take the account with Peter in prison.

**Acts 12:7-8** (KJV)

*And, behold, the angel of the Lord came upon him, and a light shined in the prison: and he smote Peter on the side, and raised him up, saying, Arise up quickly. And his chains fell off from his hands. 8And the angel said unto him, Gird thyself, and bind on thy sandals. And so he did. And he saith unto him, Cast thy garment about thee, and follow me.*

The passage says the angel raised Peter up even as he told Peter to stand up; the angel did not place Peter on his feet. Then the Bible tells us that Peter's chains fell off from his hands. God did that; prison chains falling off both hands required power beyond what Peter possessed. However, the rest of the commands from the angel could be completed by Peter: 1) Put on your clothes, 2) Put on your sandals, and 3) Follow me. In other words, God will do what only He can do, but He requires that we do what we are able to do.

Unlike Elisha, God knows exactly where you lost "it" (yourself or something valuable), but He wants you to retrace your steps and face the place. As seen in this text, God will take that walk with you. Retracing your steps oftentimes is part of your personal development. God loves you; therefore, He even cares about your losses. He doesn't care how you lost what you lost nor whose fault it was. He has that information already. He simply wants to help you get some things back. What He doesn't return, He will teach you how to live without.

Perhaps you lost yourself early in life and have never considered where or when the loss happened. Maybe your early years were healthy, and you grew up with both parents or other family members who nurtured your individuality and encouraged you to be confident. But somewhere along the way, you got lost. Maybe you got lost because of an abusive relationship, losing a loved one, a catastrophic diagnosis, the ending of a relationship, an addiction, the responsibility of caring for siblings or parents.

- Did you lose an important part of you when you married?

- Did you lose an important part of you when you divorced?

- Did you lose an important part of you when you decided never to marry?

- Did you lose an important part of you when you were fired?
- Did you lose an important part of you when you were demoted?
- Did you lose an important part of you when you were unfaithful?
- Did you lose an important part of you when you accepted continual abuse?
- Did you lose an important part of you when you betrayed a friend?

Whatever the situation, the first step is to acknowledge the loss. Take your loss to God, and spell it out. Believe that you are not talking to Him in vain. Go to God as if He really cares about your loss. May I assure you that He does? What is it that you no longer have but think you need? If you really need it, God will return it. If He returns it, don't be hesitant to embrace it. Resist the temptation to replay the loss; imagine God's pressing the resume button on your life and get busy producing.

⌒

*Lord, thank You for Your Word! You have taken such good care of us, and You continue to show us how Your Word is designed to light up our paths as we walk in Your way. Some of us have painful memories that are affecting our lives, but we have not yet surrendered to You. Help me surrender, please. I believe I will be better off, but I am afraid. Help me remember that surrender is part of the healing process. In Jesus' name, I pray. Amen.*

# Operation Meditation

1. Do you ever look in the mirror and wonder who the person is that is staring back at you?

2. Do you ever wish you could yell "cut" and start your life all over?

3. What is that you have lost? Is it self-esteem? Confidence? Your identity? Your will to live? Your faith? Hope? Love for yourself? Is it the ability to feel? Is it compassion? Is it the ability to stand up for yourself? Is it courage to face a challenge you have been avoiding?

4. Where did you lose it?

5. Who or what have you been blaming for this loss?

6. Are you willing to confess this sin to God and trust Him to help you retrieve what you lost?

# CHAPTER TEN

# How Much Is Your Sin Going to Cost Me?

THIS CHAPTER WILL explain the title of this book. At the age of 22 without a true basis for what a Biblical marriage entailed, I entered a union unprepared. I was a Christian, and he was a Christian; what else was needed? Oh, premarital counseling... Well, my fiancé and I attended one session, and the preacher placed a great emphasis on Proverbs 31. How I held on to that passage for dear life, and she became my model for a godly wife.

The premarital counseling session focused primarily on my role as a wife, and at the time, I was fine with that focus because I loved learning (and still do). In retrospect, we should have discussed my lack of identity, my need to be accepted, that real love was much deeper than I realized, my inability to set healthy boundaries, and the insecurities created from growing up in a dysfunctional home.

The time did come when I had to admit my insufficiencies and make a decision to address all these issues on my own—without a human being with skin, that is. My longing for acceptance and approval from a person placed me in a highly vulnerable position. But God, through His Word, taught me, counseled me, encouraged me, healed me, settled me, and re-directed me. Mine was a long journey, though.

In the meantime, I entered a marriage and quickly dis-covered that two halves only make a whole in math. We were both incomplete with unidentified, and therefore, unresolved issues. As a result, I endured years of infidelity coupled with mass confusion because he was not only a Christian but also a pastor. I asked him a question one day, hoping he would see how his actions were affecting me. The question was the title of this chapter: "How much is your sin going to cost me?"

This subject alone could be a book, but I have decided to make it only a chapter. In retrospect, the question I should have been asking myself was "How much am I willing to allow his sin to cost me?" I had a choice, but I was not mature or emotionally healthy enough to understand my responsibility to myself nor the role I played in this toxic combination.

*I was not mature or emotionally healthy enough to understand my responsibility to myself nor the role I played in this toxic combination.*

In 1991, we were married, and in 2000, he was diagnosed with HIV. This date marked one of the most painful times in my life; that day was dark and filled with uncertainty. An hour later, I rushed to a place of privacy and wrote in my journal, "Lord, will I ever smile again from my heart?"

Oh, I wore a smile on my face, but my heart was shattered into billions of tiny pieces. I had questions for God, but none of them included, "Why me?" I had studied the Bible and had taught too many lessons to ask this question, but I did ask, "Why this?" Like my son in another chapter, I felt I needed to remind God of all the things I had done right. I actually made a list: "I don't smoke, I don't drink, I don't know a man other than my husband, I don't this, and I don't that—as if God had let these things slip His mind. Then I continued on with my questions.

- What's going to happen to my sons?
- What's going to happen to the church?
- What will people say?
- What do I tell my family? Many of them were unsaved and I thought, *Surely, they will never turn to God when they find out about this.*
- What will I tell my sons?
- How is this story going to end?
- What did I do that caused this?
- What do You want to teach me?
- What good could possibly come out of this?
- How do I count this joy?

A few hours later, the doctor called the house to inform me of the need to be tested. I had not yet taken the time to think about myself! This unexpected call created a brand-new set of questions.

- Am I positive as well?
- How could I not be? We've been married eight years?

- Who will take care of my sons?
- How will the church be affected by this news?
- What will this do to unbelievers in my family?
- What about the unbelievers in the community?

My mind was all over the place. I could identify with David in Psalm 55:6, *"Oh that I had wings like a dove! I would fly away and be at rest."* I was mentally and emotionally exhausted, feeling as if I had been buried alive. I did not sleep at all that night; I searched Scripture after Scripture, looking for relief. I made the mistake of looking for a spiritual answer for a physical condition: I was mentally and emotionally drained. What I needed was sleep.

Two days later, I was having bloodwork done. Of course, this health scare took place several years ago, and the technology then was not like today's. I had to wait for the referral to be approved. Someone reading this book may be too young to know what this process was like. When I walked into the room, I felt as if everyone knew why I was there. Of course, they did not. The stigma I felt was all in my head. *I felt embarrassed, ashamed, sad, angry, and alone.* The lobby area was completely full, and only two names were called at a time. When my name was called, I went to the back alone.

I was 32 years old, had only been with one sexual partner, who was also my pastor, yet I was in a seat about to have blood drawn to see if I will test positive for HIV! Tears flooded my face. There were two seats in the room, and I kept waiting for the other person to come in to sit there. I anticipated the look I would receive, and my shame increased. Right before I thought I was going to lose it, I felt the presence of God in the room. I felt as if Jesus had entered the room and was sitting in the empty seat. I stared at Jesus' seat to keep from looking in the other direction and facing the technician who was filling what felt like a thousand tubes of my blood. **Matthew 28:19-20** came to my mind:

> *Go ye therefore, and teach all nations, baptizing them in the name of the Father, and of the Son, and of the Holy Ghost: Teaching them to observe all things whatsoever I have commanded you: and, lo, I am with you always, even unto the end of the world. Amen.*

As I concentrated on the words, *"lo, I am with you always, even unto the end of the world..."* the tears continued to flow but they had different meanings this time. I was no longer afraid; I was grateful.

I had to repeat this test every six months for two years, and I believe Jesus always made sure that seat beside me was empty, and we experienced it together. Lest I give the appearance of being some type of spiritual superhero, let me quickly say that I experienced a roller coaster of emotions and did not know how I would continue to get out of bed some mornings because of the weight of this dark secret. Yes, a *secret* because he did not want anyone to know.

I knew I needed to speak to a counselor to help me sort through my emotions and real concerns, but that was not part of the plan. At that time, I had a very small inner circle of three women I have known from twenty to forty years. Because we lived in different states, we spoke by phone at least four times a week, if not every day. I even kept this situation a secret from them for seven years; they had no clue. All three were hurt when they discovered that I had endured such a hardship alone.

*I am now a firm believer that nothing good grows in the dark.*

I am now a firm believer that nothing good grows in the dark. I divorced him seven years after the diagnosis; we were never intimate after his diagnosis. Every test I underwent was negative, and more than fifteen years have passed since that day when my life changed forever. I thank God for protecting me when I didn't know I needed it. As I read through the many journals that I filled from pouring out my heart to God, I see His faithful hand at work on every page.

After I was healed emotionally and mentally, God began to tell me to share my story with others who needed to hear about His faithfulness amid what appeared to be a hopeless situation. I was reluctant and only obeyed sometimes. He would not let me rest with this partial obedience. At first, I began sharing my story with individuals, but then He instructed me to share it publicly at a church when I was asked to be the women's day speaker.

I remember journaling about this opportunity too. I prayed, "God, I don't want to be known as the woman who was married to the man with HIV." I then proceeded to write the lesson that I would share, but I did not truly include what I thought was my story. However, God won, of course. I rewrote the lesson in obedience to His direction. I saw silent tears and literal tears on the faces of members in the audience as I shared a portion of what God had done for me.

Then came more questions:

- How will this disclosure impact my career?
- How will I ever remarry if this disclosure becomes public?
- Who will want to marry a woman with this history?

I surrendered. Then it seemed like everyone I spoke to—strangers and friends alike—gave me the same line: "LaSonja, you should write a book." This all took place in about a 15-year time period.

I took this matter to God because I heard it so much. I confessed to Him that I wanted control over my story and writing a book would definitely strip me of all control. My story would be public for all to see. God gently rebuked me and corrected my perspective on this story as well as my life. Hence, the title of the book: It's My Story; *It's His Story.*

**Psalm 107:1-2** (ESV), *"O give thanks to the LORD, for he is good: for his steadfast love endures forever! Let the redeemed of the LORD say so, whom he has redeemed from troubles."*

**Genesis 41:50-52,** *Before the years of famine came, two sons were born to Joseph by Asenath daughter of Potiphera, priest of On. Joseph named his firstborn*

*Manesseh and said, "It is because God has made me*
*forget all my trouble and all my father's household." The*
*second son he named Ephraim and said, "It is because*
*God has made me fruitful in the land of my suffering."*

From his birth to death, Joseph's story is one of my favorites. God has taught me many lessons through his life. My friend, his family history will prove that dysfunctional families have been around since Cain and Abel. The term *dysfunctional* is not found in the Bible, but all the traits are there. In summary, Joseph was the beloved son of Jacob and Rachel. Jacob loved Rachel; as a matter of fact, Jacob worked seven years to marry Rachel, but Rachel's father, Laban, tricked Jacob, giving him Leah instead. (The story is a must read!)

**Genesis 29:20** (ESV), *"So Jacob served seven years to*
*get Rachel, but they seemed like only a few days to him*
*because of his love for her."*

I love this verse. What a love story! The next time your spouse omplains about how long it takes you to get dressed, try telling him that Jacob waited for Rachel seven years and he counted it as only a few days! I digress, but it's important to share some background to assist with understanding the text for this lesson. Jacob was allowed to marry Rachel, but he had to work another seven years for her. Wow! This would be a real, reality show.

Rachel gave birth to two sons, Joseph and Benjamin. The Bible says the following about Joseph in **Genesis 37:3-4** (KJV):

*Now Israel [formerly called Jacob] loved Joseph more than any of his other sons, because he had been born to him in his old age; and he made an ornate robe for him. ⁴And when his brethren saw that their father loved him more than all his brethren, they hated him, and could not speak peaceably unto him.*

Can you imagine what Joseph's life was like? More than likely, he spent more time with his siblings than his dad. Perhaps you don't have to imagine what the favored son's life was like. Maybe you know what it feels like to be hated and the recipient of consistent unkind words. Joseph's problems didn't end with hate and unkind words; eventually, his very own brothers plotted to kill him. However, their plan did not come to fruition. Isaiah 54:17 (NASB), *"No weapon that is formed against you will prosper...."* When God has a purpose for your life, weapons will be formed, but God keeps His promises and is true to His Word.

*When God has a purpose for your life, weapons will be formed, but God keeps His promises and is true to His Word.*

**2 Corinthians 1:20,** *"For no matter how many promises God has made, they are 'Yes' in Christ. And so through him the 'Amen' is spoken by us to the glory of God."*

Nevertheless, the brothers sold Joseph to the Midianites, and the Midianites sold him in Egypt to Potiphar. There, Potiphar's wife became infatuated with Joseph, and when he did not fall prey to her charms, she accused him of rape. Potiphar

*While your situation and circumstance may be different from anyone you know, the God You serve has never seen a problem He could not solve.*

took retaliatory action against Joseph, putting him in prison for a crime he did not commit.

Just in case I wanted to feel sorry for myself or think that nobody knows the trouble I see, God has placed numerous accounts for me to read and remind myself that nothing is new under the sun (Ecclesiastes 1:9). This statement is not meant to minimize your pain at all; however, it is meant to remind you that you are not alone. While your situation and circumstance may be different from anyone you know, the God You serve has never seen a problem He could not solve. Jeremiah 32:27, *"I am the LORD, the God of all mankind. Is anything too hard for me?"* Remember, God's questions are always rhetorical. The answer is "Of course, not!" Nothing is too hard for God.

When Joseph was elevated from the prison to the palace as Pharaoh's second-in-command, he marries and gives his sons names of significance. Though the Bible spells out several tragedies in Joseph's life, that Joseph was not alone is evident. God was present in every scenario, allowing the plot to thicken. Proverbs 15:3 states, *"The eyes of the LORD are everywhere, keeping watch on the wicked and the good."*

Obviously, God made Himself known to Joseph, and the proof is in the naming of his sons. His first son's name, *Manasseh,* carries the meaning: "Because God has caused me to forget ALL my trouble and ALL my father's household." The word *forget*, which is *shakhach* in the Hebrew, does not mean, "to not remember as with amnesia." Rather, *forget* means "to fail to hold in mind." In other words, though you will remember the events, your focus will not be on them; you won't be consumed nor will your life be controlled by the past event or events. When God heals, He makes it possible to look at a wound, acknowledge it, and move on.

I have a scar on my knee, and I well remember that it happened while I was riding a bike. I can remember what I was wearing and even the location of the accident. While I can recall all the accounts, there is no pain involved. That scar is not even sensitive to touch, and so it is with the scars on my heart that I have mentioned in many of these chapters. I see them, I acknowledge them, but I feel no pain. *God has caused me, like Joseph, to forget.*

God didn't stop here. Joseph had another son, and his name, Ephraim, also had a special meaning. *"It is because God has made me fruitful in the land of my suffering"* (Genesis 41:52).

The Bible does not shed any light on whether Joseph was his brothers' enemy, but Genesis 37:4 does say they hated him. Hatred does for an enemy make. Yes, Joseph's pain was gone, his focus was redirected, and God blessed him tangibly. God, being the Good Shepherd that He is, prepared a table before Joseph in the presence of His enemies.

*Lord, thank You for sending Your Word and healing me. I pray now for my friend; please touch, heal, forgive, and deliver in the way You see best. I know that You always have our best interest at heart and that every-thing we go through is meant to work for our good but ultimately for Your glory. Help us to remember that You saved us to serve You, and we have no story without you. We have an obligation to glorify You with everything we have. Everything that has breath owes You praise.*

*Thank You for caring about our hurts and pains and thank You for being a very present help in the time of trouble. Help us to be like the woman at the well and share the great things You reveal to us with all those whom we encounter. Help us to remember the words You gave Peter, that after we are converted to strengthen our brothers. Give us the faith to believe that You can do the impossible.*

*Lord, we love You; thank You for loving us first. In the name of Jesus, I pray. Amen.*

Some of the Scriptures that I relied on during the tragedy God trusted me to endure include the following:

**Joshua 1:5**
*I will never leave you nor forsake you.*

**Psalm 34:4**
*I sought the LORD, and he answered me; he delivered me from all my fears.*

**Psalm 147:3** (KJV)
*He healeth the broken in heart, and bindeth up their wounds.*

**Psalm 3:5**

*I lie down and sleep; I wake again, because the* Lord *sustains me.*

**Psalm 4:8**

*"In peace, I will lie down and sleep, for you alone, O* Lord, *make me dwell in safety."*

**Psalm 5:3-7**

*In the morning,* Lord, *you hear my voice; in the morning I lay my requests before you and wait expectantly. ⁴For you are not a God who is pleased with wickedness; with you, evil people are not welcome. ⁵The arrogant cannot stand in your presence. You hate all who do wrong; ⁶you destroy those who tell lies. The bloodthirsty and deceitful you,* Lord, *detest. ⁷But I, by your great love, can come into your house; in reverence I bow down toward your holy temple.*

**Psalm 5:11-12**

*But let all who take refuge in you be glad; let them ever sing for joy. Spread your protection over them, that those who love your name may rejoice in you. ¹²Surely, O* Lord, *you bless the righteous; you surround them with your favor as with a shield.*

**Psalm 6:4**

*Turn,* Lord *and deliver me; save me because of your unfailing love.*

**Psalm 16:5-8**

Lord, *you alone are my portion and my cup; you make my lot secure. ⁶The boundary lines have fallen for me in pleasant*

*places; surely I have a delightful inheritance. ⁷I will praise the
LORD, who counsels me; even at night my heart instructs me. ⁸I
keep my eyes always on the LORD. With him at my right hand, I
will not be shaken.*

## Psalm 27:13-14

*I remain confident of this: I will see the goodness of the LORD
in the land of the living. ¹⁴Wait for the LORD; be strong and take
heart and wait for the LORD.*

## Psalm 32:8

*I will instruct you and teach you in the way you should go; I
will counsel you with my loving eye on you.*

## Psalm 24

*The earth is the LORD's, and everything in it, the world, and
all who live in it; ²for he founded it on the seas and established
it on the waters. ³Who may ascend the mountain of the LORD?
Who may stand in his holy place? ⁴The one who has clean hands
and a pure heart, who does not trust in an idol or swear by a
false god. ⁵They will receive blessing from the LORD and vindica-
tion from God their Savior. ⁶Such is the generation of those who
seek him, who seek your face, God of Jacob. ⁷Lift up your heads,
you gates; be lifted up, you ancient doors, that the King of glory
may come in. ⁸Who is this King of glory? The LORD strong and
mighty, the LORD mighty in battle. ⁹Lift up your heads, you gates;
lift them up, you ancient doors, that the King of glory may come
in. ¹⁰Who is he, this King of glory? The LORD Almighty—he is the
King of glory.*

**Psalm 34:17**

*The righteous cry out, and the Lord hears them; he delivers them from all their troubles. The Lord is close to the broken-hearted and saves those who are crushed in spirit. The righteous person may have many troubles, but the Lord delivers him from them all; he protects all his bones, not one of them will be broken.*

**Psalm 116:12 (GW)**

*How can I repay the Lord for all the good that he has done for me?*

**Psalm 145:16 (GW)**

*You open your hand, and you satisfy the desire of every living thing.*

**Psalm 136:1 (KJV)**

*O give thanks unto the Lord; for he is good: for his mercy endureth forever.*

# Operation Meditation

1.  Can you identify with Joseph or his brothers?

2.  What memories do you need God to heal?

3.  Trace the origin of your greatest pain. Did you play a role?

4.  If you were victimized like Joseph, what is your next step with God?

5.  Read Psalm 93:4. Mightier than the waves of the sea is His love for you! What comes to your mind? How does it make you feel?

# About the Author

D R. LaSonja Flowers-Ivory began her teaching career by homeschooling her sons through second grade. Later, she taught grades three and six, then earned a single subject English credential and taught grades nine through twelve. Her academic accomplishments include earning an Associate of Arts and Science Degree (Mountain View College, Dallas, Texas), a Bachelor of Arts Degree in Child Development (California State University, Northridge), a Masters Degree in Educational Leadership (California State University, Channel Islands) and a Doctorate Degree in Educational Leadership and Policy Studies (California State University, Northridge). Her dissertation focused on the Perceptions of African American Males as it relates to school belonging and academic engagement. Dr. Flowers-Ivory has served as a high school administrator since 2006 and currently serves as a high school administrator in the Dallas, Fort Worth metroplex. Dr. Flowers-Ivory is the Founder and Chief Executive Officer of Ivory Educational Consulting, LLC and Ivory Educational Publishing.

Contact LaSonja for speaking engagements at
www.ivoryeduc.com • ceo@ivoryeduc.com
469-290-4421

Made in the USA
Middletown, DE
08 July 2019